RUSSIANS AS PEOPLE

WRIGHT MILLER has been a free-lance writer since attending college at London University. He has written textbooks, has made many BBC broadcasts on Russian themes, and in 1958 he published a book for children called *The Young Traveller in Russia*. During the last war Mr. Miller was sent to Russia by the British Government, where he worked with a Russian staff to publish a British weekly newspaper called *British Ally*. Seven years have been spent in the writing of RUSSIANS AS PEOPLE, which is based on Mr. Miller's intimate knowledge of Russia and the Russians gained during visits and residence there between 1934 and 1960.

RUSSIANS AS PEOPLE was first published in 1961.

RUSSIANS
AS
PEOPLE

By
WRIGHT MILLER

Preface by
ALEXANDER DALLIN

A Dutton  *Paperback*

NEW YORK
E. P. DUTTON & CO., INC.

Preface

IN RECENT years we have seen a mushroom cloud of American writing on Russia. Some has been excellent, some not so. But virtually all the serious work has been concerned with the "system"—the political institutions, the structure of government and economy, the record of diplomacy. Only gradually has attention shifted to the informal and elusive. The great and crucial gap has been in our understanding of the Soviet people.

Students of Soviet affairs have shied away from the Soviet social scene, I suspect, because of their pervasive interest in the unique political system; because professional sociologists and anthropologists could do no conventional "field work" under Soviet conditions; because, to do a good job on Russian society required a kind of "feel" that few trained and unbiased observers possessed; and finally, because even when foreign travelers were more freely admitted in the 1950's, there was justified skepticism about the soundness of conclusions reached after short-term tours on the vodka circuit.

All this is not to suggest that many of the recent travelers' memoirs are not valid or valuable. But there was still needed a combination of prolonged exposure to Russia, a thorough knowledge of language and culture, and an ability to listen, observe, and communicate. All these qualities Wright Miller obviously possesses, and this helps explain why the present volume will be so welcome to those of us who hope to look beyond the stereotypes of Russians as good people or evil people, automatons or Dostoyevskians, ideological beatniks, uncouth muzhiks, or irretrievable Bolsheviks.

Many of the questions Mr. Miller asked himself had previously been posed in circuitous and often imaginative ways—because no direct ways of answering them were open. Thus the Harvard refugee interview project some ten years ago did important and valuable pioneering work in this field. Margaret Mead and Geoffrey Gorer were among other professionals who, without particular empathy for the people or culture, came up with challenging albeit highly controversial hypotheses. Some of these studies were genuine contributions to an understanding of Soviet reality, as well as proof that a culture could be studied "at a distance." Yet they usually required a variety of filters, lenses, and adjustments to correct for the selectivity of sample, time lag, political bias, and a multitude of other factors that made for distortion of evidence. They could not be a substitute for direct and continuous observation on the spot by men of good will and good sense like Mr. Miller.

Taking for granted the political setting—never ignoring it but assuming its existence and impact—Wright Miller sees the Russian as an individual and the Russians as groups, in ways which I believe truly add to our understanding. Given an admirable combination of sympathy and balance, he is able to comment on morals and mores with genuine insight. He points out exceptions and limits to his own observations. He buttresses his cultured and informed remarks with judicious statements by others who have written on Russia, and with passages from Russian literature. As a result of all this, I found myself captivated by this volume, and this was true even where the author and I did not completely agree.

This book has, I think, no simple "operational" conclusions to offer. It is, thank goodness, no psychological warfare guide. But it has much to teach us about the nature of loyalty and discontent in Russia, about the types of collectivism and individuality, about social classes and identities, about initiative and self-consciousness, and about the sense of "continuity" of the Russian people.

It may not be too much to hope that this book will help us better to comprehend the "Russians as People"—and also stimulate other sophisticated explorations of a similar sort.

The Russian Institute   ALEXANDER DALLIN
Columbia University
December, 1960

Contents

Illustrations

RUSSIANS AS PEOPLE

I

Introductory

The failure to recognize the truth that there are many worlds,
not merely one, is the deepest source of confusion between us,
and the most stubborn obstacle to that mutual toleration which
is the very best that is conceivable between our two societies.
Mr Walter Lippman, after visiting Mr Khrushchev in November 1958.

IN THE present period of history it seems unnecessary as well as
inadequate to regard other nations as being fundamentally 'like
ourselves'. It was once a major and often painful advance in
human development to believe people of other nations to be
of the same human stuff as ourselves—to become able to accept
the bristling, odiously-clad stranger or pagan as members of the
same human race. But now that it is almost everywhere held
axiomatic that nations and races ought to be getting on well
together, and when we are all in course of acquiring the same
atomic plants, collars and ties, analogue computers, underclothes,
motor-scooters, detergents, and so forth, it seems more important for mutual understanding that under such superficial
resemblances the differences between us—many of them the more
fundamental for being concealed—should be freely acknowledged. A nation is judged in the end by its people rather than its
power, and if this in present circumstances seems a new rather
than an old-fashioned idea, so much the better.

The Russians as people are found particularly likeable by strangers from a great many nations and especially, as a rule, by the
English. But because many of them look rather English, have a
similar sense of humour to the English, learn the same geometry
and algebra, play the same hopscotch, prefer to be free from

political police, would like more woollens and more nylons, wish little harm to their neighbours, would dash into the road to snatch a child from under a car—it does not follow that, with all this in common, they are so much like ourselves.

I have tried in this book to write about the Russians as people, not primarily as victims of Communism nor as enthusiasts for Communism, but as people *different from ourselves* who are only partly formed by Communism, and partly by the inescapable geography and history, manners and morals and tastes and traditions which, being Russians, they are born to.

They are beginning to look more like ourselves in the streets of reconstructed Moscow and Leningrad, of resurrected Minsk and Rostov. If the streets are greyer, more depressing as a rule, cruder in design than those of many cities further west, if the shops are less frequent and less elegant and the shoppers less well dressed, yet not one of these shoppers, probably, ever goes hungry, many of them own more than one pair of shoes apiece, they wear far more nylons than ever used to be seen in Russia, and a man in a good suit—though hardly yet a woman in a good suit—is no longer necessarily a foreigner. And if the expressions on people's faces seem dull to a Western visitor, they light up more readily than they used to. People will talk more readily; restrictions on contacts with foreigners are fewer or more diplomatically concealed than under Stalin's dictatorship.

If the Russians with all their indoctrination, restriction, and over-organization are slowly approaching something like the pattern and standard of life of other industrialized peoples the fact must be counted one of the major hopes for world peace. Yet there is not the slightest sign that the non-representative system of government in Russia is likely to modify its fundamental nature. The Soviet Government will apparently continue to forbid its people to form the smallest group or club except within the official framework and under the controls laid down; it will continue its refusal to trust the people to express disagreement with any line of policy except in so far as they may be clever enough to make their disagreement or suggestions look like the existing line; and it will keep in being a police system adequate to prevent these forbidden things from happening. Perhaps one should not expect any of these basic attitudes to change, since they are an essential part of the system which has brought about the increased power and prosperity which the Soviet Union now enjoys. And presumably the Soviet Government and its supporters will continue to believe that other countries must come eventually to accept their own type of distrust for political human nature as part of the necessary price to pay—the only price it is possible to pay in their view—for an industrial standard of living.

The persistence of these attitudes will not make it any easier for foreigners to grasp what Russia and Russians are actually like. Even native citizens must carry passports and report all important journeys in Russia, but it is not only government prohibitions which make the country difficult to penetrate for the foreigner. To characterize manners and traditions, landscape and climate, and the ways in which people react to them, is by no means so easy as in the case of some other countries. If Russia were by some miracle to be thrown open as freely as France or Switzerland, for English tourists to see for themselves without official interference or assistance, travelling and booking hotels under the same conditions as the natives, it is likely that they would soon forget the resemblances between Russians and English, and that their further explorations might in general prove disappointing.

One can drop a foreigner into the centre of Parma or Siena, into the old market place at Bâle, or into almost any corner of any French town, and in ten minutes the most unsophisticated will have drunk in something of the atmosphere of Italy or Switzerland or France. But there is no corner of Leningrad or Moscow where a visitor could similarly absorb in a concentrated way the atmosphere of Russia. In Russia the life of the people does not vibrate upon the air as it does in Mediterranean countries, where one does not need to know the language in order to understand much of what is going on. The Russian language does not even lend itself to a simplified or pidgin version; there is practically no halfway house for the foreigner between no Russian and good Russian.

And it is not merely the language which defeats personal exploration. One is baffled again and again by a subdued or characterless exterior, of scenery, of people, of buildings, and of behaviour, which one must suspect conceals a life to which one cannot find the key. The great grey blocks of modern flats, the endless broad streets of older two-storey houses with their un-pointed brickwork and steaming double windows, the wooden villages which seem dumped rather than rooted in the forest or ravine or steppe—they defeat interpretation, unless after long acquaintance, as completely as the streets of South London or Leeds. The people seem neither particularly friendly nor particu-larly hostile but somewhat expressionless for the most part, like the scenery which wanders away in all directions with little to catch the eye. And if occasionally the scene is redeemed by a bright new edifice, a quiet canal, a pillared façade, or the gilded bulbs of some fantastic church, or if one meets, as one is sure to do, a Russian who lights up with hospitable warmth, one feels at a loss to know whether these are accidents or whether they are at last the typical Russia for which one is trying to probe.

Russia is strange but perhaps it is not strange enough. It might be easier if one had to adapt oneself to a total strangeness, as of the desert or the tropical forest, yet Russia is not altogether unlike other countries of Northern Europe. So one finds it all the harder to believe that the generally unpicturesque and unkempt appear-ance is not accidental and somehow not the 'real' Russia. Even the national smell is unpicturesque. It is a weary smell composed, one comes to realize, of the stale dust and sweat of heavy clothing, the reek of native green tobacco, the bitter smell of black bread, the stink of Soviet soap and hair-oil, and the tarry odour of im-perfectly refined petrol. There are stale damp dishwater smells and crude oil for people's hair but never anything sharp or pungent—except vodka, and the burning cold in winter, and a certain amount of raw onion on the breath.

When one adds to all these impressions the discomforts of the average Soviet hotel and that instrument of torture the Soviet telephone, the paucity of maps, guidebooks, and directories of every kind, the continual waiting for chits and for service, and the maddening combination of red tape and inefficiency with personal willingness to help, the total effect on a free tourist could well seem the result of a deliberate conspiracy to prevent him from getting to know Russia.

The tourist goes abroad to refresh himself, to be raised if possible to ecstasy by the illusion of a new world—a new landscape created by foreign men out of a foreign soil and a foreign climate. In the excitement of the landscape he takes a short cut, or believes that he does, to the people. But in Russia the man-made landscape is more recent, more makeshift on the one hand and more institutionalized on the other than in Western countries. The effect that generations of backward peasants have had on the land has been less, and the individual mark of handicraft and shop and café—quite apart from their reduction by the Soviet régime —has always been far less than in the West. The local colour has resided, and still resides, much less in the work of people's hands than in the people themselves. External appearances, including external appearances of people, can be so misleading; superficial untidiness may conceal essential skill, and a grandiose exterior may mask poky little rooms and dilapidated staircases. Almost everything needs to be interpreted and explained.

It is one of the triumphs of Communist propaganda that it has persuaded so many of its enemies as well as its friends that everything within the boundaries of the Soviet Union has been made anew. When you first visit the Soviet Union your impressions are inevitably dominated by the new, whether you are personally predisposed to admire the energy which has run up the vast apartment blocks, the factories, and the Metro, or to jeer at their 'bourgeois' design and to pity the apparently 'regimented' hordes streaming in and out of them. You pass over the old-fashioned squalor and dilapidation to be found in every other street, regarding them at first as the mere residue of the old, presently to be superseded. After some months, however, the living influence of the old Russia impresses more and more, and not only in buildings but in men and woman. It is not merely a matter of minor social habits surviving but of fundamental attitudes and habits of mind among which, as I shall hope to show, there are some which are more than survivals; they are part of the backbone of the new.

I should like to take mostly for granted the colossal increase in national production, the sputniks and walking draglines and stereo films and tower cranes, and I should like to take for granted such facts as that for the first time in Russian history no one starves; and that there is less political liberty now than there was under the later Tsars; and that the whole nation has been taught to read and furnished with reading matter; and that this reading matter (including secondhand books) must all pass a stiff censorship; and that some minor nationalities have been given a written language for the first time; and that some minor nationalities were deported *en masse* from their homelands for many years after the war . . . etc., etc. I want to write instead about the climate and landscape in which Russians have to live, and the character and habits which have been bred by the climate and the landscape, by serfdom and peasant farming, by the Tsars and the Russian Church, and by the impact of the Soviet Revolution on all these as well as the impact of what the Revolution has itself created.

My longest period in Russia was spent in and around Moscow and Kuibyshev on the Volga, during more than two years of the war, when in spite of military restrictions and the political police there were opportunities for getting to know Russians, and even for moving about the country within limits, which have hardly yet recurred. (One Englishman after three years' residence counted three hundred Russian friends and acquaintances besides those whom he met in the course of his duties.) I made longish visits to the Soviet Union in 1934, 1939, 1959, and 1960, and I have travelled across the country from Murmansk to Batoum and from Riga to Baku, but nearly all my time has been spent in the traditional Great Russia, the European part of the Russian Federated Soviet Republic, where almost everyone's native tongue is

Russian. When I say 'Russia' I shall generally mean Russia and not the Soviet Union—not even the Ukraine, which can seem a good deal more European than Great Russia does. (On the other hand when I say 'Russians' I shall not mean merely the inhabitants of Moscow, specialized and untypical of their nation as they so often are.) It is true that about half the citizens of the Soviet Union are not Russians and object to being classed as such, but there is no doubt that it is Russians who have carried out the greater part of the task of sovietization, and it is they who have given it some Russian characteristics.

2

Hibernation and Awakening

ONE MUST begin with the winter, the greedy exhausting winter which, as the peasants used to say, 'has a belly on him like a priest'. The priest brought forth nothing from the land, but he planted himself at peasant tables and expected to eat his fill. And Winter, bringing forth nothing, planted himself across Russia as the great waster and consumer—eating away the hardwon hoards of grain and cabbage, of cucumbers salted in the pickling pond and firewood stacked in the frozen passageway, making lean the wolves who pulled down horses and cattle, wasting the fat of the hibernating bear, and wasting away the patience, the energies, the imaginations and the very breath of human beings in the stale air of the huts where they huddled round the earthen stove.

And still in fifty thousand Soviet villages, and in Soviet cities under the wail of factory sirens and the hoot of American-style locomotives Winter is the great waster and consumer, wearying body and soul for more than half the year.

In Moscow the frost begins in late September and continues without a respite until April; the last scattering of snow may fall upon the May Day celebrations. Yet the severest part of the winter, the time of twenty or more degrees of frost, is a period of no more than a couple of months as a rule in the Moscow region. It is the chill monotony of the four, five, or six months of lesser cold which makes the season so hard to bear.

The crows on the Kremlin are the first sign, the host of grey-headed Russian crows which flock in from the countryside to roost among the spires and gilded bulbs until the spring. Every branch is bare already, and out in the fields only an occasional dandelion still shines among the dry stalks. Then one morning these last flowering things have crystallized, as it were, into ice overnight, and for six and a half or seven months there is no green thing but the dark fir trees. The noonday sun may still strike warm for a few weeks, but until mid-April there is not even a bud to keep the memory of fresh green alive.

November is a black month of icy rain and sleet, and one longs to see the first snow. It comes but it does not stay, and traditionally it should fall and melt again three times before it comes for good. In a mild winter it may not stay until December, and the wait is dreary. But when it comes at last the whole city seems warmed into life with the sparkle of the new dry snow, the cushioning of traffic noises and softening of echoes, and the cosy little rise in temperature which follows a snowfall. For a short while it seems as though one had entered on a more benign season instead of a grimmer one, and strangers exchange remarks as though it were spring—'It's here! It has come!'

But the sparkling vision doesn't last. A grey pall hangs far too often over Moscow; there is no changeable seaborne weather here. There are long, still, grey spells and long, still, blue spells, but few—mercifully few—gusty intervals. One misses the lively air of Western Europe, yet if the winds were to blow as they do at home, life out of doors would be impossible in winter. And so the grey pall hangs and hangs for weeks without descending in snow again, the white crests on walls sink to a city drabness, and even the sugar-caps on the Kremlin towers turn dull as the sheet of cloud above them. In the streets snow is soon trodden into slabs and knobs of dirty ice, and one must walk gingerly everywhere, keeping an eye open for little boys who dash through the crowds at top speed, striking sparks as they cross bare patches of flagstone on their single skate tied up with string.

Slipping and stumbling one goes, and the winter eats up armies of labour to keep city roads usable. In the most important avenues bulldozers attack the snow at once, pushing it into great heaps to slip down the sewer manholes which are left open and unguarded. In lesser streets and yards the house-porters, or *dvorniks*, stack up banks of snow until by the end of winter there is barely room for a car to pass. If no more snow falls for a long time, drab bands of sweepers attack the city ice with pick and shovel and pneumatic drill. The points at tram and railway junctions must be kept clear day and night, and this work, like so much unskilled work in Russia, is done by women. Muffled in padded clothes and grasping iron stakes in their clumsy gauntlets, they stand bowed and patient witnesses to the incubus of the winter.

In the worst weather it is so cold that it seems to burn. You launch yourself out of double doors into the street and you gasp. You narrow your shrinking nostrils to give your lungs a chance to get acclimatized, but you gasp again and go on gasping. Ears are well covered against frostbite, but eyebrows and moustache grow icicles in bunches, and sweat runs from under your fur cap and freezes on your temples. Presently a tickle, and the longer hairs of your nostrils have become rigid with ice. Another moment, surely, and the whole nostril will freeze over: in a panic you warm your nose with your glove, but the nostrils do not freeze, and you go on warming your nose and stinging cheeks with your glove, and you go on gasping. Half an hour's walk gives you the exercise of an ordinary afternoon. The only relief is a warm blast from the exhaust of a passing lorry; it is impossible, you think, to bear it all for long, but you can and do. You grow bolder and discover that flybuttons can be undone without calamity, even in sixty degrees of frost.

In fact you are surprised to find how life goes on in Russian towns, except during the blizzards. Cars and lorries bump along without chains, rolling the ice gradually into waves and hummocks, and over these the battered single-deck buses run as usual, their overloaded behinds giving out an occasional squawk of protest as they scrape against the biggest of these obstacles. Sleighs have all but disappeared from the traffic of cities, though the peasants' lean and frosted animals drag one-horse sledges into market still, and nearer Asia one is startled to see them drawn behind a shaggy two-humped camel. There are hand-sleds for shopping and odd jobs, and a few babies are pushed about in prams mounted on runners, but otherwise there is only the silent shuffling of the crowds in their winter footgear.

Even if you have the money it is no use trying to look neat if you are outside for long in winter; nothing will keep frostbite from your toes except the clumsy felt boots called *valenki*. These are simply right-angled tubes of felt closed at one end, and you must wear them several sizes too big, after you have first wrapped your feet and legs in strips of cloth rather like puttees. For short journeys goloshes pulled over shoes will do, and some people stretch outsize goloshes over the feet of their *valenki*, not to keep out the wet, except for a short period in spring and autumn, but to keep out the cold. During most of the winter it is far too cold for the snow to be melted by any human warmth inside a felt boot; if you stand still the cold slowly freezes you through felt and rags, more quickly through goloshes, and quickest of all through leather, which in very severe weather itself freezes and becomes useless, as the German armies discovered somewhat too late. The only effective alternatives to *valenki* are the soft skin boots worn with the fur inside—a Siberian invention called *oonty*. Air pilots sometimes wear them, and with the tops turned down to their ankles they shamble along looking like clumsy shire horses.

In the cities dark woollen overcoats are common nowadays, with a rare Persian lamb or squirrel, an occasional shapeless bear or coon-style coat probably worn by an actor, and quite a sprinkling of homely sheepskin—greasy yellow coats with the fleece inside, coats with tattered fleeces bobbing on the outside, and long cloaks for watchmen trailing right down on the ground. Many Russians must still keep themselves warm in winter with quilted cotton, for cotton is cheap and mainly home-grown, while wool is dear and largely imported. Outdoor workers may wear a quilted cotton tunic, 'Norfolk' style, in grey, black, or khaki, with a belt; the man tucks his trousers into knee-length felt boots, and his wife wears a tunic and boots exactly similar, with a drab scrap of skirt to satisfy Russian ideas of decency rather than to add extra warmth.

So, a bundle on two bundled legs, one must go shuffling and stumping through the city winter, scheming to avoid waiting in the open air, banging in and out of double swinging doors and treble swinging doors, leaving everywhere a trail of steaming breath and sweat, queueing always to park your coat, hat, scarf, gloves, and goloshes, and queueing half an hour to get them out again. It is a very indoor life behind the double windows gummed all round with paper, and an Englishman soon suppresses his desire for more fresh air or lighter clothing. Sometimes the outside air can be allowed into rooms for a little while through the *fortushka*, the little inset double window, but the foreigner, tempted by a milder spell, who reopens his whole inner window will get not only a room which may take a day to heat up again but an outer window which will stay frosted over by his own rash breath for the rest of the season.

The winter light filters in poorly through the deep recesses of the double windows. They are small enough, so as not to cool the rooms too much, the rooms themselves are usually small for the same reason, and even the window recess is half blocked by the winter store of cabbages or the evergreen plants which are among the few Russian household gods. Common among these is the aspidistra, and it sorts well with the plush tablecloths, the little rooms overcrowded with furniture, the lace-covered pillows on the high beds, and the general indoor stuffiness.

It is dark, too, for so long. Moscow's daylight is an hour less than London's in mid-winter, while further north there are only a few hours of whitish day round lunchtime.

It is long and dark and dull, but winter in the towns is tolerable so long as there is wood for heating, or so long as one is connected to the underground heating system which nowadays, in some cities, causes melted trails along the streets the winter through. It is a bracing, vigorous cold outside, not like the insidious English damp; you can puff out your cheeks and fight with such an adversary. The stale and sweaty life indoors breeds feverish germs, and yet if I went out in winter with a touch of flu upon me I would generally feel that it was the infection and not myself which came off worst from the tingling cold. On the whole, if one has not to stay outside too much, and one has ordinary food, fuel, and warm clothing, it cannot be said that the winter's cold is the worst of burdens for the shuffling masses in the streets and in the Metro.

But out in the villages—and quite half the population of the Soviet Union live in villages—life in winter is more its grim and ancient self. The open country is an icy white desolation. White mist—a crystalline veil of air-suspended ice—hangs in the near distance, and only a mile from the village you would be swallowed up in a swirling white world. There is not a stir in the silent air, but your eyes dazzle at the particles and they seem to swirl. The steely air gnaws and bites at your cheeks, a stiffening of frost aches at the corners of your eyes, and presently out of the padded silence the lightest of winds stirs the surface of the snow, lifting spicules of ice into white wisps and trails, and suddenly it whips one of these across your face like a razor-slash. You turn your back only to meet a stinging slash from the other quarter, and if you must stay out in these conditions your ear-flaps, peak-flap, high fur collar, and a gloved hand together will seem a feeble shield. And this is but the lightest of winds. Every illusion you may have had about enduring Russian cold is undone by wind, and a five-mile-an-hour breeze has a grip like an iron mask. Twice that speed is already a blizzard. Windy weather is frostbite weather, and with ten degrees or more of frost, and a moving air, one must watch for the white, bloodless patches or, in the ghoulish phrase of the medical book, 'Spontaneous amputation may supervene'.

This is the weather which ravages peasant faces, giving many of them an immobile, flattened appearance all the year, or leaving them with zigzag ears and nibbled noses which heal in clean new skin and come to look like deformities and not the wounds of winter. Somehow the peasants get their sleds to market, their scrubby little horses, their patched clothing and their expressionless faces coated indiscriminately with hoarfrost; far out on the aerodromes girls in shaggy ground-length coats keep their positions for hours at a time, flagging the planes in and out with their cheeks stung to a bright orange; on the yard-thick ice of the Volga men patiently sit or lie, blue-black with cold, dangling a line through the hole they have forced with stakes and saws; and during the war men lay in frozen snow from dawn till nightfall and then attacked the enemy in a searing blizzard.

Russians are connoisseurs of cold. There is always some place further inland, they allege, where the cold is more intense but drier and therefore more bearable. Kuibyshevites in Moscow complain of the miserable fifteen or twenty degrees of Moscow frost compared with their sparkling Volga cold, but Siberians in Kuibyshev shiver uneasily at the local thirty or forty degrees and boast of the really stimulating sixties and seventies of their home. Further into the interior of the great land mass the snow is not deeper; there is in fact less of it, there is more sun, and the air is drier and more crackling. In the strange uninhabited region of the north Caspian the snow is a mere sprinkling upon the surface of the brown earth, and one wonders to feel such iron cold.

But the land can be lovely when the air is still. On such days, under a sky which at last is blue, the glittering land calls forth that generous feeling of unlimited space which the Russians call *prostor*. ('No *prostor* in the mountains', said the old priest who was sent to the Caucasus for his health; 'You couldn't see a thing for the mountains!') On such days I would step outside and fancy, from the delicious tingling in the tips of my nostrils, that the crisp air smelt of something new; there was nothing in this frozen world to launch a smell upon the air, and so it seemed that the air itself had the smell of ozone, the pungent smell that only electric sparks can generate. Some of my happiest memories of Russia are of ski excursions in such weather—long swinging runs on the flat with Russian friends singing together, or still afternoons with apricot clouds turning rosy in the sky, when I explored the Moscow forests with only the toes of my skis ploughing ahead for company.

The fir forest is uncannily, dangerously beautiful in winter. You slip in among the white-clad giants and at first there is no sound. The drooping tips of branches wave you gently in, and then when they have got you they seem to hold up witches' fingers to warn and threaten. You start suddenly as a load of snow slips down at your back; you could swear no wind had stirred but the long finny branch had made a gesture of its own accord, a gesture meant for you. Further on a nodding giant beckons you again, and you are wrapped deeper in the spell. You stand in a white space with seven ways leading into it, and anything coming by any one of them—any magpie, fox, or foreign soldier, any lynx or wolf or witch or bear would be unheard. You turn uneasily, suppressing a wraith of panic such as you never felt in summer: there is no one there but the dark giants in their cloak of deathly white, white-clad giants with a core of primitive fear. They stand in enchanted silence, the lords of the Russian winter: to worship them as demons would not be hard. . . . And then you break a twig and see the green underskin and smell the resinous green smell and you know what they are for. They are the symbol of eternal life, the Green Man, the New Year Tree of promise, to be hung with gifts in towns.

The fir tree in the house at New Year means more in Russia than it can in countries without snow. For Russia has neither holly nor ivy, and the evergreen is not something to be fetched in for its uncommonness; it is a major part of the ancestral landscape, the green house in the woods translated into the little houses which man has made. The Christmas tree, the *yolka*, has been adopted into Soviet life as the New Year's tree, but long before it was the Christmas tree it had powerful ancient associations.

It was to the fir tree that men owed, and men still owe over more than half of Russia, their shelter from the grip of *Dyed Moroz*—Old Man Frost. Not their first shelter, for the primitive Slavs had no more than a covered hollow scooped out in the ground—the *seni*—where they cowered round an open fire. The Germanic tribes taught them how to build their hut, the *izba*, round an earthen stove which solved the problem of internal heating. And for centuries now the Russian house has consisted of these two, the *izba* or log hut and the *seni*, no longer scooped out but a covered passageway which provides a space with double doors for keeping out the cold. The size of a log hut is regulated by the length of the serviceable part of a fir trunk—perhaps fifteen feet in central Russia—and the *seni*, a store for tools and firewood, extends in a rather ramshackle way along one side of the hut, with the outer door at one end.

Inside a good *izba* it is stifling. Every chink is stopped with rags or moss, and the living space between the rough wooden ceiling and raised floor is even less than one would expect. The long wandering flue often smokes, and the accumulated breath of a large family, of smoke and heavy clothing, bed, cooking, stored food, dog, cat, and cockroaches takes a little getting used to. At least one can be grateful that the peasants no longer shelter farm animals inside the *izba* too. Everything centres round the stove, but few huts can afford the upright tiled Dutch stove; in most of them the fire is contained in the *pechka*, a home-made thing of brick or clay which may be no taller than a couple of bookshelves and little wider, but which serves as fire, oven, drying table, bench, and even bed. And still without a tall stove it is never warm enough in the worst weather, inside the *izba* or the double-windowed cells of town flats, or the leaking little frame houses in the suburbs. To come through so many thicknesses of doors and curtains into such a fug, to be stuffed into such a little choked and steaming chamber and still be cold—it gives some inkling of the impotence and despair generated through centuries by the Russian winter.

Among my Moscow friends was a writer of peasant origin— we may call him Dmitri. His enthusiasm for village life throughout the year was a byword in his circle, and there were amused headshakings when I accepted an invitation to spend a winter day with him in the one-roomed *izba* which was his home. Thanks to a train service of quite unusual convenience Dmitri was able to double the parts of Moscow novelist and chairman of a collective farm, and so I was able to make the journey of sixty miles at the cost merely of three hours each way on the bare slats of a stopping train.

I descended from the stinking warmth of the train into a wind like sandpaper, but in half a mile found the chairman's hut easily enough, since, like everyone else's, it bore his name under the eaves, and pushing in with a scarified face I was hardly surprised to discover my host in bed. A lean and hardy hunter of wolves who was accustomed to lie out in the snow waiting for his quarry, he nevertheless, like millions of other hut-dwellers, spent much of the winter in bed to keep warm, shifting his couch now and then to avoid the dripping ceiling. His old grandmother, the *babouchka*, was bent over the soup on the little stove, and I was given a narrow bench hard up against it. Between the table, bed, stove, cupboard, and piles of belongings it was hard to see where else I could have been put. There was a dank chill in the air, but at least my back was warm. Presently when Dmitri got up, excusing himself for remaining unshaven, the old lady made the bed, put back its antimacassar-like trimmings, and there was a little island of traditional neatness in the general confusion, a tiny equivalent of the English parlour. Then she laid the meal, with many apologies for its simplicity—pickled ridge cucumbers and tomatoes, a great bowl of soup which was mostly cabbage but as rich-seeming as minestrone, a dish of chanterelles dried in the summer and now resurrected with potatoes in the frying-pan, the inevitable *kasha* of large-grained buckwheat also fried, and hunks of good brown bread. We admired the bread, the damp, whole-wheat and whole-rye 'black' bread; flour in this village was not spiky with chaff, as it was in some places. We admired the fuel which had baked it—the much-loved birch, best of all woods for burning, and itself smelling, when the log is newly opened, of refreshing newbaked bread. We admired the brass bedstead; in the war, in the district to which the old lady had been evacuated in the Urals, people still slept on the old Russian 'shelves' of bare boards. We admired the translation of the *Jungle Book* from which Dmitri's son, now at the university, had first learned of the English. Then Dmitri plied me with peasant sayings and Armenian brandy while the *babouchka* plied us with glasses of Russian tea—three of us to two glasses, endlessly replenished with tinted water without milk or lemon, but always steaming from the samovar, till what with the stove and the tea and sheer animal heat the hut began at last to seem warm, the sweat stood out in beads on all our foreheads, and the old lady passed round a napkin and smiled because we were enjoying a real winter *chai s polotentsem*—'tea with a towel'.

But this of course was a feast. One of the drawbacks of Russian life from the stranger's point of view is that he can never escape a feast, or not until he has become a very frequent visitor to a Russian family. The embarrassments of being the honoured guest are swept along on a great sea of the generous Russian nature, which has the gift of being able to meet you confidently at once, like a good handshake, and yet to preserve a reticence and even diffidence appropriate to a new acquaintanceship. This is the pervading atmosphere of Russian people, not the importunate curiosity nor the roaring chumminess of some other nations. It is hard to seize and yet it is the very breath of Russia. It can be so powerful that, if you feel at all in sympathy, it almost blots out the poverty of surroundings and inhibits one from discussing or even noticing them. It is an atmosphere which the English generally find congenial, but it is also one of the non-political reasons which make it difficult to 'find out', in Western material terms, 'what the country is really like', even when one is being received into the very bosom of ancient Russia.

So on this occasion, in the intimacy of a most traditional Russian milieu, it was not at all easy to ask, as I wanted to, how the ordinary days and nights go by in winter. The old 'hungry gap' in spring has probably gone, but as to occupation, a collective farm has no more jobs to offer in winter than any other farm in a cold climate. Those in charge of animals must feed them, some peasants study, some have lectures or films organized for them, and some make the old-fashioned spoons and toys of varnished wood, which are regular items of trade in the market. But for many, apart from fetching in firewood, dipping a saucepan into snow for water, and dashing to the lavatory hut with its throne of yellow ice, must it not, I asked, be much the same old state of semi-hibernation through all the worst months of the year?

Under the brandy's influence Dmitri broke into his recently-acquired English:

'In the winter', he said, 'the peasant come and say "Dmitri Ignatievitch, there is a fox who eat our hen. Take your gun and shot him." And I take my gun and shot him. The peasant come and say, "Dmitri Ignatievitch, there is a *wolf* who eat our *horse*. Take your gun and shot him." And I take my gun and shot him. The peasant come and say, "Dmitri Ignatievitch, there is a BEAR who eat our COW. Take your gun and shot him." And I take my gun and shot him. But in the night, in winter, I like that very much. Then I am sitting, with one, two, three, four, six, eight, ten, twelve glass beer before me and I am *thinking, thinking, thinking*!'

After the middle of February Russians know the worst of the cold is over, and in March the sun becomes warm enough to melt a little snow each day on sheltered roofs and sills and pavements facing south. Soon the streets begin to run with streams of thaw, though at night these turn again to treacherous sheets of ice. Almost every ceiling drips with water, and the porters climb on to the roofs with their aluminium shovels, hurling down masses of snow to compete with the natural avalanches which slide off with a noise like trains approaching. The nights are white with the mist of meeting thaw and frost, the incautious foreigner leaves off his heavier clothing and gets bronchitis, and in the misty dark one trips and falls full length over a new kind of obstacle—great cylinders of ice six inches in diameter, which have at last dropped out of the battered downpipes where they have been collecting all the winter. In April peasants bring pussy willow into town, and in a few more days the *rasputitsa* will begin—the appalling state of 'roadlessness' when all outside the towns is mud and icy slush and flood, when villages for a short period are completely isolated and neither sleigh nor cart, lorry nor tractor can stir.

There is one lovely aspect of the thaw, on stretches of open ice such as the Volga. When winter began, the river froze in chaos and travail, its waves suddenly arrested as they rose in the icy wind, and the ragged blocks then packed together in impassable ice-jams. But the snow fell and made all smooth, and now the whole mass, long since turned to ice, may thaw in a peculiar way, leaving a crust which freezes every night, and underneath it a structure like a transparent meringue, resting on a foot or so of the deep firm ice which still covers the river. The crust, thawing and freezing by turns, frets itself into filigree shapes and veins like mineral growths, and eventually separates into oval plates of filigree, each one borne on a frail pedestal of deliquescent rods and threads of ice. As you walk across the Volga there is a hushing noise all round as one by one these structures collapse, and the plates subside and disappear in the pools on the gently undulating icefield.

The icefield itself is becoming lucent and honeycombed beneath, and soon there are broad channels at each side of the Volga and no one now attempts to cross. One morning at ten o'clock you look out and see thawing channels and the grey ice-plain, and then at twelve you look out again and the whole Volga, as far as you can see, is a blue loch reflecting the April sky. Soon sheets and fields of dirty ice come down again, whole prairies and steppes of ice, solid sometimes for a mile together, then loose floes carrying abandoned huts and barrows from three hundred miles upstream, then all is packed ice groaning together, then again the blue of the loch, and after that again more fields of ice.

You can go out at last, well booted for the mud, but after the snow there is only ugliness and disillusion—disillusion at the dead and yellow flattened grass, and the revolting heaps of garbage now appearing from under the snow where they had been thrown all through the winter. The only green things to be seen are the harsh leaves of autumn-sown wheat, and perhaps, after all, the spring is to be as disappointing as the blackened growth around a Lancashire town, or brackish as the tops of the Pennines.

And then, suddenly, it is warm and it stays warm. In ten days it has changed from grey ice and snow and slop to tender green, and the boys are bathing in the pools.

Spring is a cascade once it has begun. There has been no slow growth of buds on mild days, no lambs' tails in January nor colts-foot starring the wastes in February or March. There has been no flower or bud at all, and now everything comes in a rush—catkins, coltsfoot, anemones, violets, celandine, and apple blossom all together. The flowers are nearly all familiar English ones, but they crowd together so unseasonably that it seems as though the Russian season were not harsher but milder, juicier, more scented and abandoned than our own. All the new seedlings, all the green growths from last year's buds are swift, the ground is flooded with soft shoots, and one tramples on a foaming softness in the fields. At the end of the Metro line, where one went skiing a month ago in the half-wild Sokolniki Park, the ground now shines faintly in the May nights with dog violets, and the forest at another Metro terminus, Ismailovo, is carpeted with wood anemones like the Forest of St Germain. There are no primroses, no daffodils nor bluebells in Russia, but the flower to gather in armfuls from the forests is the lily-of-the-valley. Peasants bring dripping masses of wild flowers to sell in the centre of Moscow— lily-of-the-valley and cowslips, lilac and sweet-smelling creamy orchids, solomon's seal and the golden globe-flower, which we must go to the mountains to find in Britain.

The queen of the flowering trees is not the hawthorn but the bird cherry (*cheryomukha*), a softer thing with trailing flowers more waxy and bridal than the may, nestling among the leaves instead of drowning them in blossoms. And the other peak of the Russian spring is, surprisingly, the lilac. Too luxuriant, one would have thought, to survive the cold which even the haw-thorn cannot endure, it stands all through the winter, and the scent of lilac on old country estates and of *cheryomukha* in the forests make the romantic spring of Russian poetry and novels.

The double doors and windows are open at last and fastened open, and in the cities the barrack dwellings are alive with a sense of relief from something of the round of six-day toil, of queues and shortages and endless making-do. The family will get out of its single room at least into the sunny streets, and if a river or a lake is near, the women may do their laundering there on Sundays instead of in stifling conditions at home. The streets are bright with cotton frocks and clean white shirts—overwashed and under-ironed for the most part, but a refreshing contrast to the padded winter jerkins now thrown open, in which a few must still trudge through all the months of heat.

In the leaning wooden suburbs men sit on doorsteps with jam jars full of greenish beer, and further out the shack-dwellers scratch out little kitchen gardens, fenced in fluttering sheets of waste tinplate stampings. For those who are better off the annual *villegiature* begins, the migration to the little wooden frame-houses or *dachas* where thousands of families spend the summer, leading a simple country life, bathing and stocking up wild berries, mushrooms and honey against the winter. As for the peasants, they are already fiercely engaged in the summer's toil— the ploughing, seedtime, haymaking, pasturing, and harvest which must all be crammed into four or five months of ceaseless labour, under a sun which can reach a hundred degrees and more in the heat of the day.

Nothing in Russian life is more dramatic than this leap from muffled winter into summer. Life behind double windows is transmuted into life with windows wide open, and out in the sunshine there is a swarming around building sites and over roofs, a hurling away of rusty ironwork, a blossoming of sky-blue tramcars, and a coming alive of walls in cream and pink and buff and grey and green.

In the countryside every stream must be bridged afresh, each year, as soon as the spring floods subside. For in this land of a million waters there are few metalled roads and only they, as a rule, are carried on permanent bridges. Elsewhere the dirt roads are roughly patched in May to make approaches to the crossings, fresh piles are driven into the river bottoms, and rough-hewn bridges with rattling floors are built on top. Sometimes a convenient unit of the army does the job engineer fashion, but otherwise the peasants must improvise in the ancient way, unless they prefer—with or without the approval of the local Soviet—to continue splashing through a ford of perhaps a hundred yards in width, until in five months time the ice returns.

On the great rivers which are too wide for any but the rarest bridges, on the Volga, the Dvina, the Dnieper, and the Don, on lesser rivers which are unknown to Europe and yet each one greater than the Seine—on the Khoper, the Vetluga, the Bug, the Desna—at dozens of points the river crossing must go through the same laborious stages year by year.

At Kuibyshev, for instance, city of a million people on the Volga, it is simple enough in winter to get over to the rural right bank. There is a long island and a secondary channel, the Volozhka, but both this and the main Volga are frozen deep. The only man-made contrivance you need is a little humpbacked bridge over the first few yards by the city, where the steaming discharge from the factories keeps a channel ice-free all the winter. Often I crossed this to brave the fourteen hundred yards of ice in a blistering side-wind, scramble up the bank of the long island, plough through half a mile of snowy tracks across the island, and slither over the ice of the Volozhka and so up a steep little cliff to the overhanging huts of the first village. Then in spring when the Volga thawed at the edges the passage entered its second phase, and to cross the widening channels you had to wait for clumsy little rowboats which had been dragged out of their winter shelter in the hope of earning your rouble.

Later there could be no crossing at all among the crashing sheets of ice, and for a week or so the rural bank was entirely cut off. The brown flood-water followed and gave way to green, the rowboats took a few passengers across, but for most traffic there was no way until, after many rumours, the ferry pier was at last made good from winter damage. Now a stocky tug appeared, towing a raft ready to bear a mass of peasants wedged among cartshafts, lorries, stovepipes, animals, and dung. Persons not dressed as peasants were invited into the cleaner atmosphere of the tug, and for us the voyage was pleasant round the tail of the long island, though it took as long to reach the village this way as it did on foot in winter. But this was only temporary. Soon the water in the Volozhka began to fall, and the tug changed its course to fight upstream the whole length of the island, rounding its head and gingerly descending the far channel in a three-hour voyage with the inevitable result, before long, of sticking on a sandbank all night. Then the ferry settled down to its summer service, shuttling between Kuibyshev and the near shore of the island, which we were left to cross on foot, wading the Volozhka at first until the villagers had rebuilt their bridge. In autumn the bridge comes down, the tug retires, the Volga freezes, and the whole cycle begins again.

From Kuibyshev to the nearest railway bridge over the Volga is eighty miles, to the nearest road bridge is several hundred, and it may always be thus. Yet the villages on the right bank must turn to Kuibyshev for their mail and all but elementary supplies, the villages on the left bank opposite Kamyshin must turn to Kamyshin for theirs, and so it must be for a thousand communities along the Volga, the Dvina, the Dnieper, the Don, the Khoper, the Vetluga, the Bug, the Desna. . . .

Every summer between two and three hundred thousand persons are employed in river transport—'subject to sufficient depth of water', as the time-tables say—and every autumn most of them must turn to other jobs. For almost every Russian, in fact, the autumn is just such another season of violent, brief activity as the spring. Before the end of August the slogans go up: 'Gotovit' k zimoi!' ('Prepare for Winter!') Enormous stocks of logs are laid in, stoves and central heating must be made to work, the double doors rehung, the double windows sealed again, chinks in the sun-dried woodwork stopped, and the eternal leaking Russian roofs made good against the snow.

In villages and suburbs men patch their own huts, but in town the winter preparations are the responsibility of the house committee in each block, and ultimately of the *dvorniks* attached to the yards which are the centre of residential life. The house committee may call on other help, but to judge by newspaper reports their efforts are often as ineffectual as the meeting which I attended one evening in my own yard in Moscow. It was a warm Saturday in August, and the agenda, 'Winter Repairs', scribbled at the foot of each staircase attracted only a handful of tenants. We waited for forty minutes and then broke up for lack of a quorum. The promise to reassemble was never kept, and some of my neighbours suffered a long time, that autumn, before their flats were fit to stand the weather.

In September the temperature falls with drastic suddenness, and in the countryside the rains bring on the second annual round of slough and mud—the autumn *rasputitsa*. As soon as this is past, battues of wolves begin, against the season when hunting is impossible.

The city-dweller may read of the wolf-hunts with a comfortable thrill. For him the trams and buses still run, and there is no change from creaking cart to soughing sledge. And yet for town and country alike the fierce sequence of the Russian seasons is inescapable. In summer there is relaxation for most townsmen, and for the peasants unremitting toil. But in spring and autumn there is for everyone the feverish adjustment, and then through all the winter, in spite of any modern alleviations, the capacity simply to endure. Winter eats up breath and energies in merely keeping alive. The snow lights up everything at first and invigorates the atmosphere, and if the weather is not too cold people of all ages may go out to ski, but after the first relief one is reminded too dumbly of other interminable winters—a formless and inescapable burden like the shawls of old age.

Winter dims and slows everything down, drags you into the sealed life indoors. Children under two are kept inside all through the coldest months, and the older ones, when the thermometer sinks below minus twenty centigrade, are sent home from school. Their elders hurry from one shelter to another, for those who stand and gossip soon find their feet begin to freeze. The ice penetrates even indoors; in the bare anterooms and waiting-halls where a good deal of Russian life is spent, the woodwork is glazed over with the frozen breath of those who huddle waiting for their pass, their permit, their allotment, their redress, or merely their train which winter has delayed. In the biting air outside, ungloved fingers are skinned and bleeding if they momentarily touch metal. Stocks of every food must be protected from the cold, and even potatoes must travel in heated trains. The handling of every kind of goods becomes clumsy and slow, and every year bales and crates, stacks of sugar and stands of timber are ruined as they lie under the snow. In spite of every prohibition there is an exodus of workers from outdoor jobs, and trains are sometimes cancelled because engine-drivers refuse to leave the shed.

The part played by the Russian climate in forming Russian character has often no doubt been exaggerated. Russian introspectiveness has been put down entirely to the effects of the Russian winter, imprisoning men in the mists of their own souls; or alternatively the huddled winter life has been held responsible for the Russian emphasis upon relations between man and man rather than between man and the world of objects. The solitary family, it has been said, or the solitary individual-in-his-own-right could not be bred in the Russian climate, or if bred could not survive. Yet the Finns, in a climate scarcely less severe, had bred just such individuality as early as the sixteenth century. The medieval Finns had lived in patriarchal 'great families' similar to the Russian, though somewhat looser; but by 1520 almost the whole of Finland was divided among individual freeholding peasants, who lived as a rule, and for choice, in farmsteads widely separated from each other, while in Russia the shackles of serfdom were still being fastened more and more firmly upon the villages.

Yet although climate cannot be considered a sole cause of a system of social relations, or even of a penchant towards introspection, that is not to say that it isn't to some extent involved in their origins and in the reasons for their persistence. And especially perhaps in Russia, where Communist propaganda has led so many of us, whether Communist or not, to look only for the economic or the political, it can be useful to consider other, ancient, formative forces.

For if foreigners sometimes make too much of the influence of the Russian climate, this is partly because the Russians themselves have been—and still are—obsessed by it. Much of the American Middle West is colder in winter than European Russia, and yet the Middle West has earned no worldwide reputation for cold. The first Middle Westerners came mostly from countries more advanced than Russia, and from countries with climates more benign; they took it for granted that they would impose their own pattern of life on the country and on the climate as far as possible, and industrialization has enabled them to continue this mastery. But the Russians, though they fathered a few ingenious devices such as felt boots, did not begin until very recently to master the effects of their climate as the North Americans did. The Russians were a backward people, in industry, in agriculture, and in education, they know they were backward, they know that they are still backward in some respects and they fear they may be so in others; their past backwardness is an inextricable element in their present. And the climate has played a part in that backwardness, along with serfdom and the repeated invasions and the despotism of the Tsars. The climate mattered *because of* Russian backwardness, and it encouraged habits of labour and of life which were bound to persist when the Bolsheviks began their assault upon the climate and upon the miserable, monotonous poverty of the world of objects. There were at first no habits to live by other than the old pattern of dumb plodding interspersed with furious bouts of activity, and the old tendency for too many people to help at peak times, as at harvest, while for long intervening periods individuals dribbled along as best they could.

These alternations have been one of the most distinctive features of Russian life, typical not only of work habits but also of Russians at leisure—in the preference, for example, which they have usually shown for luxury rather than comfort, for the occasional feast rather than a steady standard of living. (Other reasons than climate, of course, are involved in the origin and persistence of this characteristic, and some of them will be discussed in another chapter.) The steady, less exciting tempo of modern industrial life has in the last few years gained a great deal upon the old passionate methods, and the even more recent improvement in living standards has begun to induce a more comfortable pace in private life as well. But any unusual conditions still bring out the old 'surge' methods; students still try, in spite of admonition, to 'take their work by storm'; and the country has a long way to go yet in preparing more smoothly for spring and autumn emergencies, in building more permanent bridges of steel and concrete, or in constructing more permanent roads which could take wheeled or caterpillar vehicles all through the year.

The villages do their sowing earlier than they used to do, fires are lit under lorries for winter starting, there is far more outdoor sport in winter, hardy swimmers plunge into the Moscow River when the air temperature is $-4°F$, less hardy ones plunge into the steaming open-air pool heated to $77°F$—the most vigorous section of the nation do their best to behave as though winter wasn't there. But still the coldest weather burns, and people must huddle inside, out of the rasping wind. . . .

Long endurance of the Russian climate has bred some conventions and attitudes which have embedded themselves in Russian behaviour so that their origin has become forgotten. There is the convention, for instance, in regard to outer clothing. Winter garments are so dusty and cumbersome that no one could think of keeping them on inside a house. As a result it has become bad manners, at any season of the year, to retain any outdoor clothes indoors for however brief a time, and when the theatres were barely heated during war winters we were still obliged to leave our coats, scarves, gloves, hats, and goloshes in the cloakrooms, clinging to our seats thereafter and hardly able to keep our teeth from chattering during the performance. The cloakroom habit, the treble swinging doors, the treble entrance halls and long passages to keep out the cold—they all make it almost impossible for one to 'drop in' anywhere in Russia. Winter is a serious matter, and winter still helps to make life serious all through the Soviet year.

3

The Russian Scene

BY MAY the traveller can get out at last—out away from Moscow's stark concrete and long bedraggled streets of yellow.

If he goes by air he sees the emptiness of the land, the forest but little broken for hundreds of miles west and north, and the settlements, once outside the Moscow region, scattered at first no thicker than in the New Forest, and then as thinly as in the north of Scotland. The line of a railway is rare, the line of a metalled road rarer still, and the villages dribble along two or three miles of earthen track as though distance and pattern were of no account.

England is packed with intimate shapes so that from the air it is a chaos; France, less crammed, has beautiful forms; but Russia is so empty that one longs for some shape or pattern on which to rest the aeroplane eye. Only towards the south do the chimneys and coal-heaps of the industrial Ukraine show something like an English density. Beyond them the land is drier, the villages are few again and the farms more huge until they give way entirely to sunbaked pasture and at last to desert. But except in these southern regions there is water everywhere. From the air the land seems splashed with the dark patches which mean water— ponds and dams and ragged lakes, rivers of infinite tributariness, scimitar shapes cut off in river sands, floodings in green meadows and seepings in peaty bottoms. The most dramatic features— almost the only dramatic features from the air—are the great scooped-out bends of rivers like the Don.

The aeroplane, however, is a poor way to see the country. It flattens everything to a map, but from the ground one discovers with pleased surprise that most of the land is not dead flat, not flat like the Fens or Flanders. As the train rolls at a lulling speed across Russia, the landscape heaves gently up and down and breaks into a variety which only after a long time acquires a monotony of its own. There are long passages of airy birch and twisted oak, thickets of silence under the fir trees, dirt roads slithering into valley bottoms, moon-daisies on sandy banks, green rye and poppies, a wooden hut with a nesting-box high on a teetering birch-pole, then dark heaths and peat mosses, blue flax and beet, cabbages and sunflowers, rye and young wheat, the long slow arc of a downland cutting, a village forested with nesting-poles and TV aerials, a factory on a river-cliff, a blue-painted onion spire, and again dead fir, green forest flashing with magpies, young wheat and potatoes, and always the rivers—brown forest streams, shallow shingly wastes, great sandy ox-bows, steel bridges being built under guard, and the slowing down to a crawl, under the scowl of the sentries, on the longer bridges where the horizon opens out into limitless blue. There is horizon, and there are small scenes repeating hour after hour, but never anything so clear as South Downs or Côte d'Or to mark the landscape, never any dramatic passage from one zone to another.

Only at last in the far south, at the end of the Ukraine, is there the dead plain and the heat-haze distance which one had expected. Then after Rostov, rolling through land with no heights but a rare Mongol burial-mound, the train rises gently, gradually, towards the distant Caucasus. Yet still it rises through a dead straight landscape, so that the whole earth seems slowly tilted, and the horizon of corn cuts the setting sun at an angle. But this is not strictly Russia, not the land that formed most of the Russians. In the old Russia there is only the modest landscape repeating, repeating, like folk-songs with never a final coda.

In Western or Southern Europe flat land is mud or sand which dried out during a period counted in geology as only yesterday. But in Russia the flatness is mostly far older, and different because it is older. It is not often the flatness of fat and smiling farmlands; for great expanses of those one must go to the steppes of the

Ukraine. The Russians have more usually had to scrape and husband and force their tillage where they could—from burnt forest or rockstrewn lands, from thin coverage over chalk or gravel, or from black patches among the peat.

There were mountains far back in Russian geological history, when the early rocks folded—'folded gently' is the description—into ranges, but these were slowly eroded by the seasons. The seas of later periods flooded them with sediment and retreated again, the rivers silted their valleys, and the last ice age, grinding down south as far as Kharkov, wore away most of the heights that remained. When the ice melted it left behind the low scattered ridges and piles of glacier rubbish, the moraines which make so many of the patternless little elevations of Russia today. Geologically speaking, Russia is a land which is almost 'finished', yet it is also starting again. For the ice ground out new depressions as well as levelling the hills, and in these depressions new streams have dug themselves deeper since the ice retreated. So that Russia today has been described as 'a country where few bits are higher than other bits, but a great many bits seem to be lower'. The most typical feature of Russian scenery is now the ravine or gully. Even in the south, where the land at first glance seems laid out with a spirit-level, it is cut up by hundreds of small ravines, as the Germans outside Stalingrad found to their cost.

So Russian scenery is full of small surprises. In the undistinguished rolling country south of Moscow, suddenly there is the shallow river Pakhra, curving its way past diminutive limestone cliffs at the old estate of Dubrovskoye. Westwards through the forest one descends to find the Moscow River winding by little red sandstone bluffs, and to the north, in fir forest without an undulation, the trees break into desolate clearings where granite leans out of the soil, like a scene in New England.

Thirty miles from Moscow, or even half that distance in some directions, is far enough for one to reach the wild.

One Sunday morning I went down to Moscow's water-port at Khimki, intending to go as far as local transport would take me on the lakes of the Moscow-Volga Canal. How far this might be was no question of time-tables, it appeared, but a typical Russian matter for argument between the crowd on the landing-stage and the captains of the waiting boats. There were, it was alleged, no boats. Or all the boats were reserved for excursions. Or no boat could take all of us. But eventually, as so often in Russia, the knot of conflicting requirements, the tangle of incompatible tentacles emanating from a dozen authorities and organizations was suddenly cut by a human common-sense decision, and we were all squeezed on to a single white *bateaumouche* whose skipper, with a gesture which implied that he was breaking all the rules, consented to take us as far as Tishkovo.

His vessel, named with unnecessary modesty *The Little Bee*, was a slender frame constructed in some fit of Bolshevik tempo around a diesel engine so powerful that it threatened to tear loose from its bearings. For the greater part of the voyage the engineer sat hard on the most vigorously bouncing corner of the engine mounting, as we screamed across dead waters and by quiet forest shores with a shrill whizzing vibration more unendurable than that of any aircraft. However, I had hopes of Tishkovo; anything with 'tish' in Russian implies peace and quiet. By degrees the *dacha* people were cast off at shaky little piers to visit their green frame-houses, and when we approached the end of the longest lake there was but a handful of us left to step ashore on the single plank which served Tishkovo. The unbearable engine was suddenly extinguished. The throbbing in our ears was pierced by the fluting of birds as they shot across the green spaces round Tishkovo, which was clearly, in spite of the building of the canal, the same tiny, faraway forest settlement that it had always been —a few brown huts with fir trees towering all about, and beyond them great grassy avenues rich with wild strawberries. My fellow-passengers disappeared into the hamlet to bargain for country food; they had only a couple of hours before the *bateaumouche* returned. But my stomach turned at the prospect of another three hours of the *Bee*. In eighteen or twenty miles to the north one could reach a well-served railway line, and though I had no map—for there are no tourist-scale maps for civilians in Russia—yet on this bright day there was the sun to steer by, and indeed the broadest avenue pointed north.

It was a poetic walk at first—to be making one's way in the silent summer forest without habitation and without another traveller. The dead-straight avenue drew one deeper and deeper into a vegetable silence that was almost unbroken. A squirrel ran across, a jay creaked once or twice, and then all again was a continuity, a silent procession towards the cupful of light balanced on top of the infinitely far-off pines. Imperceptibly the avenue closed in, the gloom grew deeper and the track became faint, but the direction remained. The direction remained but all unnoticed the track grew fainter still, and then there was no track at all and only the merest impression of a direction—an impression left perhaps by beasts but not by men, or not by men for many years past. It seemed to lead, if it led at all, through gloomy, threatening jungle, down into a great basin of dead and leaning trees, still overshadowed by standing giants above, and singularly like the scene of a popular Russian painting of a family of bears at home. The sun was quite shut out, and one peered nervously at every breath and crackle in the dark underforest of spikes. I remembered the Russian expression 'bears' corner' to describe somewhere far away from the world, and I remembered too that bears still haunt the north of the Moscow Province.

There was no other track. One could but stumble through the dead forest, snapping off branches and repeatedly deceived by the ghostliness of light ahead. After a long time the daylight opened on a melancholy clearing—yet no man's clearing but a waste of lichened rocks patched with heather and juniper, and the forest soon closed in again. Another rocky waste followed, of the same ancient, sad appearance, like the approach to a Bois Dormant, and it led indeed to a tumbled stone barrier shrouded in thorns. But this was wild rock, and beyond it only more juniper and the dismal firs once more. There are few ancient ruins in Russia; one does not have the sense of treading on layers of older human settlement. But the ancient forest harboured such distorted rock erections, such tumbled arches and fallen scaffolds of hairy trunks, such nests of mystery under the dead branches, that I began to feel the power, and a little of the fear, of the Russian folk legends which grew from them. If no human hand, then some other thing or power must have been stirring to leave these uncomfortable and distasteful forms behind. One did not need to believe in trolls or spirits of the wood in order to feel that one was treading among the work of strange dead hands, malevolent hands surely because so meaningless in what they had left—the paths that always ended in a silent thicket, the rock which was never the wall or gravestone or gatepost that it appeared at first to be; as one drew closer one always knew the rock could never have been any of these things and yet it must have been something, something neither of nature nor of conscious man, as disorienting as the shapes in a surrealist painting. The silence was harder to bear than the cries of strange birds or the lumbering of animals would have been, and for two dark hours I tramped with an ever-growing uneasiness that night would find me still caught in this patternless web.

I kept, or thought I kept, a rough direction, and at last quite suddenly, on a path no more promising than any other, the silence was laced with a gentle tinkling of bells and the piping of a reedy flute. Goats came stepping delicately through the pine-needles, and behind them a sallow goatherd, piping five thin notes to keep his flock from straying. He had gathered wild raspberries in a clean white bucket home-made, like the pipe, out of birch-wood, and there was little about him but his shabby suit to recall the present. But if he was the herald of some more primitive region he was a distrustful one. His inexpressive Russian countenance showed not the slightest surprise at meeting a stranger; he seemed to have no desire for conversation, but with three morose words pointed to a trail which would lead out into the fields of his little village.

It was more primitive than anything I had seen, rather like something from an old Russian engraving, with its sandy plots of bluish, stunted rye, huts scattered haphazard round a shallow ravine, and a wooden wellhead where the women in white kerchiefs were drawing water for the evening. Except for the barred and gutted church there was no visible sign of the changes of the last thirty years. The barefoot women passed no greeting; I was from another world, and they were even more pressed to get their supper than I was to find the right road before dark.

A muddy track from the well plunged into the forest again, but more hopefully than before, and soon it gave way to the logs, laid not long since, of a corduroy road where two great lorries came bouncing and bumping. But they were loaded with prisoners who grunted derision as they returned from the timber-cutting; they were giving no lifts to anyone. As they disappeared into the dusty twilight the corduroy became a sandy avenue between the fir-trees, broad enough for sixty men to march abreast, but not another vehicle nor person appeared. Dimly it stretched straight and straight ahead, in a silence no longer frightening but as unbroken as in the forest itself. The darkness became so intense that one could continue only by keeping one foot in the ruts and one eye on the stars, and still for eight miles there was no sound of man or cart or hut, only the dead-straight track. But the firs rolled back at last, and a copper moon rose through a warm dusty air scented with hay, over fields still glimmering with scythemen. The avenue grew broader than ever, it opened into a crossroads as large as a parade-ground, and there to the right were the shacks of a settlement. Deep in dust and sleep, it showed a single light above the planks of a rickety station, and within ten minutes I was on board a late electric train back to Moscow.

In days of freer travel I visited the deep country much farther from the city, and by 1960 I could even buy medium-scale maps of central Russia. The elements were always the same—patches of forest and patches of field, stumpy felled forest fiery with willowherb and the summer haunt of the wolf, countless meandering streams, and muddy tracks trickling from village to village. Over great areas there were no *points de repère* but these.

A determined and resourceful outlaw, one felt, could still make his way across a great deal of Russia in summer, avoiding main roads and railways, keeping himself alive on wild foods and peasant charity, and never stirring more than an occasional mesh of the governmental net.

Even in wartime, when all travel was almost unbearably difficult, I had Russian friends whose chief delight it was to get out every week-end in summer, exploring by compass, sleeping under the stars or occasionally on a peasant's floor, carrying bread and cabbage and making soup over a campfire, and surpassing in every way the endurance shown by the wellfed foreigner.

On many occasions we kept to the rivers, bathing in pools at deep horseshoe bends, sometimes sleeping by fires which we made in the sand, and waking to the cries of seagulls. For the river and the forest—the green forest for preference, not the fir forest—are the best of Russian scenery. The Moscow River, only ten miles above the city, is as fresh and fringed with flowers as the Thames above Oxford, a river that can recall *The Scholar-Gipsy* or some poems of William Morris. And the long lagoons and the water-meadows by the Volga, patterned with swathes from the haymakers' scythes, they are jewelled, 'enamelled' as the Elizabethans used to say, enamelled with a Pre-Raphaelite brightness in purple and yellow loosestrife, white waterlilies and arrowhead, forget-me-not, buttercup, meadowsweet, and the pink stars of flowering rush, and all with a lavish freshness and lucent green which the slower English season cannot equal.

The fir forests, and the swamps and moors which alternate with them—they make a Northern summer like that of the Scottish Highlands, not a mere attenuation of the season further south but a different summer, wild and free and full of game birds, dark and even forbidding in its ground tone, but blossoming in its own startling way. The mystery lies not so much in the dark impenetrable masses of forest and the long brown monotony of moor as in the stark contrast—the magic which brings forth white waterlilies on every bronze pool, sows the moor with tiny violet flowers, and sends flights of swans rising against the black fir. The Swan Lake is not the artificial ornament of some Tsarist

Rambouillet; it is the wild lake to which you might penetrate in a lonely hunting expedition, after a day's march over the crickling pine needles. The swan is a wild bird of the north, an image of wild nature at its most powerful and lovely; it is the image, in the ancient epic of Prince Igor, for the thoughts of the bard winging forth to tell his tale.

The steppe is quite another thing. It makes you want to roll on your back and kick your hooves at the blue bowl of the sky. Sometimes from Kuibyshev we took a journey to nowhere in particular, out into the immensity of the steppe—not the tall waving grass of the virgin steppe, for that has gone except in a few inaccessible parts of the south, but the vast fields and pastures and fallows with never a hedge, and the bountiful sense of space to spare and to waste. The cream-coloured fields sparkled in summer with dry, silver-haired flowers—bugloss and cornflower, larkspur and corn-cockle—and the green tracks, fifty yards wide and more, rising and falling gently under the vault of the sky, led us on in an ardour of liberty. So fine and clean was the Volga air that summer smells carried over immense distances, and the scent of the wormwood steppe was borne over a mile of the river, right into the city of Kuibyshev. Once on a May morning we found ourselves walking into an inexplicable but unmistakable odour of coffee. There was not a hut nor a person to be seen, there was nothing apparently but the open landscape to generate this un-Russian odour, and we speculated about coffee-scented herbs and coffee-scented earth until we came over a rise to a peasant woman lugging a sack ahead. It was a time of great food shortage, when coffee was almost the only commodity which could be bought freely. Shouldering her store of this valuable tea substitute, she had laid its scent into the air like an animal leaving its trail, and the aromatic particles had hung suspended for more than a mile in the still dry sparkling morning.

The space and the wild—they are the background of the Russian scene. To an Englishman it can be a delight to lose himself in miles of forest which no hand has planted, or to wander in a green solitude heavy with the odour of *muguet*. It is a green peace with a dark, monotonous undertone. It produces a sensation caught to perfection in Chagall's painting, *Le Poète Allongé*, which hangs in the Tate Gallery.

And yet, in spite of these delights, it has to be admitted that to the closer eye the Russian scene is for the most part disappointing. Once you have drunk your fill of the prodigal, untenanted distances, and once the ecstasy of spring has hardened into the formless fluttering of summer, then you can hardly fail to find the nearer view lacking in shape and feature. Except for the absence of mountains, the scene is made out of much the same elements as in England or Scotland, but they seem to fall into neither a familiar pattern nor an exciting new one. There are little scenes for connoisseurs who can make their own scenery, but even these pall after a while because over long distances they simply repeat. There are a few rather melancholy themes, such as the line of thin fir trees touched in with a Japanese brush at the edge of the landscape, but there are few dramatic outlines and few intimate corners. The 'typical' Russian scene is either an unpaintable vastness or something like a bad Corot, a Corot of the later facile manner without even the manner, so to speak, or else perhaps an undistinguished Harpignies or Theodore Rousseau. The only word, in fact, to describe much of the Russian scene is 'unkempt'. Poor in striking natural features, it is a natural disorder into which agriculture and forestry still seem largely an intrusion. There has been so much land to spare, and agriculture was so primitive for so long, that the face of Russia has not yet been worked over and transformed as the land has been in Italy or Belgium or Britain. Americans and Canadians often feel more at home than Europeans do in the Russian landscape; the patchy central regions remind them of Illinois or Indiana, and the south, with its heat, and the air vibrating like a corn-chandler's, recalls the prairie. The man-made quality typical of the West European landscape is in Russia only beginning to arrive.

And if the landscape is still largely unkempt, the works of man in the landscape are scarcely less so. Nowhere, or almost nowhere is there any sweet shape of cottage or garden, any cosy village corner or lovingly-decorated porch, canal boat, or cart. There is no popular art of gardening. Sometimes there is the accidental quaintness of the tumbledown; the strange leaning angles of buildings and fences, in the designs of the Diaghileff-Chauve Souris period, are no great exaggeration of the real thing. When buildings are of wood, and frequently burnt down, there is little chance for them to record the wear and habit of everyday use or the slow history of their accommodation to the landscape: what they record is the savage contrast of the Russian seasons, and the poverty and fatalism which so often left and can still leave things leaning, untidy, and all but unserviceable. Still at slippery ferry approaches or rickety bridges which might be bettered, the peasants shrug their shoulders and say 'It's always been that way'. The very names of the villages, like Vypolzovo ('The Crawl-Out'), and Chornaya Gryaz (Black Mud) can express their hopeless history. But the most significant name, and a common one, is Niegoreloye—'Unburnt'—the village that escaped burning in the Napoleonic invasion or one of a hundred other conflagrations of the past.

So they straggle, the Russian villages. The fear of fire overcomes the native liking for community, and the little *izbas* are spaced far apart, four times their own width, along the great green tracks. With their doll-size gardens no larger than the huts themselves, their unpainted logs cracked and seamed by frost and sun, and their only decoration the fretted eaves which fringe roofs and tiny windows like wooden lace, the older huts would seem, if they stood alone, fit scenes for some uncheerful fairy tale. But they repeat and repeat, facing each other across huge tracks that put the whole village even more out of scale. In many a village there is no natural centre, not even a muddy space by the church. The village market is strung along a patch of dirt road, where women and children stand patiently or squat, offering a chicken, a paper of green tobacco, wild berries by the tumblerful, and drinks of *kvas*, the native drink made from fermented bread and apples. Under centuries of serfdom the village meeting gathered in the open air, and there was little incentive to make a communal centre or to leave any communal mark upon the settlement. And today the school or 'co-operative' store or village Soviet, if there is such a building, is often just a larger hut somewhere in the general straggle. The emptiness among the houses and the wearisome scattering—they intensify one's impression of the diffuseness, the elusiveness, and the inaccessibility of Russia, to a degree which lavish peasant hospitality can never quite remove.

There is no rumble of occasional traffic through these villages. Roads are of earth, and the creaking little carts which use them are lower and smaller in the wheels than a coster's barrow. If one pair of ruts is worn axle-deep the peasant jerks his undersized horse out and ploughs a fresh pair. In summer, when the road is seamed with water, and the tractor makes long lakes among the geese gobbling in coarse weeds, there may not be room for a single person to pick his way dryshod. The women and children go barefoot, carrying their shoes in their hand as they go to market, and on Sundays a gaggle of youths and maidens, some in long boots, some without, link arms across the whole wide way, singing to a few notes played on the traditional accordion.

In the post-war reconstruction thousands of Russians built themselves *izbas* with their own hands in the old manner. The state lent them money to buy timber and the few bits of metal and glass they needed, and the rest they did with their axes, hewing the logs to size and hacking the rough jointing, for the peasant axe, skilfully used, is chisel, hammer, plane, adze, and often saw as well. They had neither time nor tools to be neat or to cut the traditional fretted eaves and bargeboards. After surviving one post-war winter in a dugout shelter, after returning in fact to the primitive *seni*, it was the height of comfort for several million families in the devastated areas to have an *izba* of their own, or even a single room in a long government frame-house.

In the steppe country house-building can be easier still, for the traditional huts here are of sunbaked earth. With floors scooped out two or three feet deep they are snug for heating, and the earth provides material for the stove itself. Outside they are rounded over like dun-coloured igloos, and it is startling, as one walks by, to catch sight of the tops of brass bedsteads and new wardrobes through windows only a foot or so above the ground. On a windy day, with rain streaming over the empty plains, the whole settlement gives the impression of swimming along half submerged in the steppe.

The mud villages are at least enlivened with an occasional coat of white or yellow wash. But elsewhere one pines for contrasting colour against the monotonous summer green and winter white of Russia. Why should there not be the vivid blues and reds of the wooden buildings in other Northern countries such as Sweden or Finland? The bold designs which flower on whitewashed huts in the South are not Russian but Ukrainian; the Ukraine endured little serfdom compared with Russia, and preserved a much more powerful tradition of independent proprietorship which is by no means yet suppressed. But in Russia the link with the past seems all but broken. In 1954 'Specimens of the Traditional Building in the Middle Volga Region' were thought worthy of an illustrated monograph, and the author, I. V. Makovetsky, noted that only a few of the elaborate log-houses, in this generally prosperous district, were keeping up the painting of their adornments. In the usual Soviet village the little cots extend in drab procession, undecorated most often except for the statutory piece of tin bearing the house-number and the occupier's name. Only from time to time a more contemporary kind of house-pride shows itself in a decent log-hut or frame-house soberly painted green or grey and carrying the neat label—'Property of Skvortsov, D.M.', or 'Pirogov, I. I.', or some other Russian Brown or Robinson.

The contrast, the lightening, of the repetitive Russian scene comes but rarely. If the church is still in use, its five domes are painted an ecclesiastical blue, and sometimes there is the glint of new gilding on an old spire, or the sowing of heavenly stars upon the blue of the onion-shaped domes. The contrast in the fat shapes concentrating, as it were, to thrust their exquisite golden needles into the sky is lovely.

Yet these domes do not punctuate the Russian countryside like church steeples in Western Europe. The medieval churches of clean white stone are uncommon survivors in Russia, and one makes expeditions to see them—to see, for instance, the famous arcaded erection at Kolomenskoye just outside Moscow, or the dumpy little twelfth-century church with its fat wooden bell-house at Zvenigorod among sandy hills like Surrey's, or the perfection of the early one-cell church on the River Nerl at Vladimir. In the late eighteenth and the nineteenth centuries there seems to have been as great a flush of church building as in Britain. The countryside in many regions is dotted with tall bell-towers, prettily washed in pink or cream, which might have been designed by disciples of Wren or Hawksmoor. Later in the nineteenth century there was a medieval revival parallel to the English Gothic Revival, and a revival which missed fire quite as often. The brick-and-glazed-tile Gothic in our industrial cities can easily be matched in Russia by churches with traditional arcaded porches, long, low, clinging and constructed of ugly brick, churches with bulbous domes of brick, reconstructions in brick of what medieval craftsmen hewed in wood or stone, and bronze plaques of raised lettering in a revived Old Slavonic script as difficult to read as the Gothic which one finds on Late Victorian drinking-fountains.

Sometimes the pillars of a Palladian frontage relieve the land-scape, and a Palladian front in Russia need not be white or cream, but just as likely pink or slate or sky-blue or Indian red. These are the old manor-houses; built from the late eighteenth century onwards, they almost without exception had these classical fronts, though the whole house might be made of creaking timber. Today, when they have been converted to institutional uses, the pillars of their porticos are still renewed, but only as hollow cylinders of plywood.

Manor-houses got burnt, however—accidentally or through peasant revenge. They are much less frequent than the *château* of recent erection in France, and the older kind of *château* scarcely exists. Russia is a country without castles, unless one is to include the Kremlins, that is the citadels, of Moscow and a few other old cities. Instead of castles there are the old monastery buildings, and some of these in fact were the strongpoints which would have been erected by kings and princes in other countries. Massive stone forts, they guard the approaches to Moscow, and many small towns are dominated by them. In the Moscow region a great white monastery with blue and gold spires stands aloof above Zvenigorod; at Serpukhov two huge southern-looking bastions front the broad valley of the Oka; at Khotkovo the old village is a little street between white gate-towers, as cosy as a bit of Ludlow; and the town of Zagorsk seems to this day no more than an annexe to the high red walls of the famous monastery, which enclose such a fantasy of old spires and domes, such Italianate halls and pink Copenhagen towers that the place often serves as a ready-made set for historical films. A mile from Zagorsk is a late red brick monastery of Old Believers, as Victorian as St Pancras Station, and in Moscow and Leningrad dilapidated monasteries still stand in every district, converted into tenements. Almost a hundred monasteries remain to the Russian Church as seminaries and for other purposes, and since 1946 their land and buildings have been free from government taxes, but little else remains of the privileged days when Zagorsk, for instance, was called Troitse or The Trinity, and the high-walled monastery was master of a million serfs.

In the monasteries, the manor-houses, and the churches, a visible thread of Russian history is kept in being. But it is a slender thread. There remain a few quiet museum-towns such as Uglich or old Jaroslavl, but other Russian towns, as a rule, have no memorials of the past earlier than the mid-eighteenth century, save a cathedral perhaps, and maybe a stone-built priest's house or the town house of a nobleman, and occasionally an earthwork as at Dmitrov. Often even these relics were levelled in the first excesses of the Revolution, though nowadays they would probably be restored and preserved.

So almost everything in a Russian town is recent; and yet, as you come in from the country you pass the whole history of Russian domestic building in review. The oldest types come first, and the further you advance into the city, the nearer you come to the present day. As you plod along the great earthen highroad the first dwellings are the shacks, the dugouts, and the *seni* improvised as they were a thousand years ago, and inhabited here by the recent migrants, the deported, or the unfortunates of doubtful status who have had to build their own shelter. There are single persons or even couples living here in shanties smaller than many an English chicken-house. After these you pass the long trail of *izbas*, bearing numbers probably into the thousands, and then the larger frame-houses, two-storied wooden chalets with probably a family to each room. Their little double windows are full of green plants even in winter, and summer brings out a window-box or two. The sidewalk now becomes a dilapidated boardwalk and presently a long stretch of brick, Dutch fashion, with the road metalled, at last, in large square cobbles. There is an air of decayed respectability about this section; one would not be surprised to see an Ostrovsky heroine reaching a white arm out of one of the larger houses to water the carnations. And then the nineteenth century follows in earnest—the two-storied stucco avenues that yawn on and on in styles of the mid and later century which are as typical of Russia as the earlier nineteenth-century stucco is of France. The shops begin now, but half of them are boarded up for dwelling-houses, and down the side streets you see dismal lines of ragged brick, dark red or hideous white. The climate plays havoc with the mortar, the joints of the brick-work are almost never pointed, and of all the shabby, uncared-for blocks of Russian dwellings the brick streets are the most depressing.

A Russian town can be anything from four to eight miles across, but if your feet have carried you the whole way in, you come at last to the uneven asphalt of the town centre, where the huge windows of Soviet stores alternate with peeling blocks of Art Nouveau frontage. The Palladian façade of the former noblemen's club survives beside concrete flats and an ostentatious mansion built by some sugar or wheat millionaire of the nineteen hundreds, while perhaps a stark new opera house or theatre looms in polished granite, uncompromising as the tomb of Lenin.

The general impression of nineteenth-century shabbiness is not, of course, continuous; there are blocks of rusty concrete flats dumped among the *izbas*, and stretches of hastily run-up factory buildings inside high fences, guarded by an old watchman with bayonet fixed, and dogs inside yelping on a chain. There is, too, the complication of a curious feeling in summer. You had expected Russia to be backward, and in respect of the huts and the dingy industrial-period brick you were not wrong. You may have expected something 'Northern', yet in spite of all the indoor life in winter the appearance of Russian towns does not seem—at least to an Englishman—to suggest the climate. There is nothing of the sad solidity of cities like Gothenburg and Aberdeen, but a strangely Southern aspect once the snow has melted. The nights are warm and short and full of footsteps, and many miles of streets are cream or pink with low-pitched roofs of Italian red. The red is in fact the rusty iron sheeting used to resist the snow, but the effect resembles Southern tiling, and so the rooftops of Leningrad in summer can recall Milan. Looking south down Moscow's Gorky Street, between the Kremlin and St Basil's, there is a horizon of golden haze over red roofs, on any fine afternoon, promising exit to the summer, the south, and the Ukraine where the acacias stand listless in the burning sun.

The summer impression mingled with northern granite, peasant grey, and modern concrete makes Russia all the harder to 'place'. But whatever else you feel as you explore the enormous streets and squares you will surely become weary of the Russian spaciousness. If it is inspiring in the countryside, it can become depressing when transplanted into towns. The grandiose effect is part of what makes old Leningrad one of the most beautiful cities in Europe, but when buildings are poor and low one is merely disheartened by the ever-present distances. Frequently the traffic skirts around vast unpaved spaces which are either unused or merely sprinkled, on occasion, with a peasant market.

The space is too huge; it diminishes human beings, and yet the original intention was not to diminish them against all this emptiness but rather to dignify them by its grandeur. If the spreading of

Russian towns began as a protection against fire, it often became, after the impact of Peter and Catherine and Alexander, a positive and megalomaniac assertion of what man could do. The inflated distances were a revulsion from the medieval crookedness and corners, from the heavy little churches, and above all from the cramped *izba*, as well as a determination to go one better than Dresden or Versailles. They intensified a contrast which has never been got out of Russian life and which seems never likely to be got out—the contrast between the grandiose luxury of the country's dominant buildings and institutions and the cell-like monotony of the mass.

There are not many intermediate grades, and to a Westerner it all seems, whether old or new, to lack almost entirely the individual touch except at *izba* level. After the long drab street frontages and the shops with their black glass fascia boards— 'Shoes', '3rd Bakery', or 'Russcentrwine No. 1'—one longs for the smartness of a little private-enterprise pharmacy or coiffeur. Yet even before the Revolution the Russian street was never so diversified as the shopping streets of Western Europe. Merchants liked, if possible, to have their stores together for security, in arcades or great buildings like the Gostinny Dvor in St Petersburg which could be well guarded at night.

The rarest kind of erection in Russian towns has always been the single-family dwelling-house. A *kottedj*, as they call a house of the English or German type, is an expensive unit for Russian conditions, difficult to heat, and although the Soviet régime has produced a number of such houses, they are concentrated in a few places only, largely to serve the new intelligentsia—a handful near the Pravda building and others at some of the prettiest spots round Moscow, at Ussovo in the forest, or the 'writers' village' at Peredelkino.

Town life in Russia is tenement life, still usually at a density of one family per room, the room itself of no great size, and its amenities generally the barest, with cooking, washing, and lavatory accommodation to be shared at the end of the corridor with other families. I visited an old man once on a second floor in

Trubnaya Street, a dilapidated nineteenth-century street in the centre of Moscow, whose cell-like home was entirely of bare, worn brick; walls and ceiling were brick and the brick floor welled up into a stove on which he slept. In the new concrete blocks the accommodation is still often of the same tree-trunk dimensions as the *izba*, and some people have to occupy such rooms without an outside window. The concrete cracks, the stucco falls in lumps, and the whole building is permeated with the stale damp smell of Russia.

Only in the later 1950's have blocks of three- or four-room flats begun to be at all numerous. So it has been a relief to be able to get out of one's rabbit-warren and drink in the grandeur of the old Empire buildings in their washes of pink, grey, cream, slate-blue, and maroon, or the sculptures in the Metro, or the uncompromising new office blocks, or the grey concrete of the tall flats on the broad new *chaussées* leading out of town. They call forth some real satisfaction in their contrast with the slatternliness of most Russian living conditions. And now that Russians are beginning to have some prospect of better housing for themselves, they have not given up all their sense of public display, of participation in the grandiosity. One remembers the merchants in old Moscow who built themselves mansions with two or three halls of ballroom size, while the ordinary life of the family went on in a row of small chambers upstairs.

The broad Russian scene has often enough been cited as the origin of the 'broad' Russian nature, but it would be quite as plausible to argue the reverse—that it is the Russian character which has contributed a good deal of its own spaciousness to the landscape. It was not inevitable that Russian towns and villages should be so strung out; in some countries people have clustered their wooden houses together in spite of their fear of fire. It was not inevitable that the Russians should echo the monotonous breadth of their countryside when they built their cities; they might as naturally have crowded everything round the warm and intricate life of a *piazza*, in a reaction against too much *prostor*. It was not inevitable that the Russian peasantry in their backwardness and their *prostor* should have developed their rather loose communal organization; they might equally well have sought security in a society of small, highly conventionalized units like those of the great plain of China.

And yet, if the roots of Russian 'breadth' are to be sought in the complex of Russian history and institutions rather than in the landscape, that is not to say that geographical influence has been negligible. The Russians had a suitable landscape for their 'broad' nature to expand in, and when people have established a man-made landscape on the basis of what nature provides, it becomes for them a social norm, and the part played by nature is easily forgotten. 'Spaciousness' in all its implications is still taken for granted by the Soviet Russian, perhaps even more than by his ancestors; it is left for the outsider to question whether things would have been different if the broad Russian nature had tried to expand in a land divided by high mountains, or in an area as densely populated as Java.

The sense of undeveloped land and resources, along with other historical factors, still helps to encourage in both governors and governed the Russian feeling of unlimited potentialities and the megalomaniac assault upon nature and upon circumstance.

A large proportion of young Russian men have always wanted to go off and chance their arm in a new job or a new district when spring came. The land itself has never offered barriers; its bound-lessness inspires and draws on the spirit of youth. When the land-owners had thrown out the Mongols, Tatars, Poles, Lithuanians, and other invaders, it was they who created the barriers by tying men to the soil as serfs in order to get it tilled. But during the three hundred years of full serfdom the peasants never ceased to believe that the land by right was theirs, and they knew that there was always more land, further off, to be had for the taking. In the century from 1550 to 1650 or so, whole villages used to desert *en bloc* from an overlord they could not stand, and even after the imposition of penalties which made serfdom complete, the hardier types continued to disappear into the unexploited lands of the South or Siberia. After the freeing of the serfs in 1861 the tramp, the wandering labourer, and the hauler of river barges were a regular feature of the Russian summer, and under the Bolshevik Government the workers still expected to be able to move casually from job to job in the old way. Today the nomadic impulse has been mostly funnelled towards the cities, but it is much alive, and until the passing of laws which from 1938 until the end of the Stalin period tied people to their jobs, it caused a fantastic turnover of industrial labour.

It is partly because of history, partly because of Communism, but partly also because the land is so broad and open that what is most dynamic in Russia tended, and still tends, to emanate from the centre. There were few physical boundaries which could generate local autonomies; and although regional loyalties might have been expected to arise as a matter of convenience in such a huge land, they did not grow up, except at a low level, because those who ruled Russia did not wish them to.

What is magnificent, what is clean, and particularly what is new in Russia—from the Dutch barns and the English stud cattle to the Moscow University and the little electric train which transports books in the Lenin Library—is almost always the work, ultimately, of the centre. What is dirty, old, hole-and-corner, tumbledown, may also often be the work of the centre, but more often it is the work of the individual—the individual, that is, at the level of everyday anonymity, not the heroic level at which the Government exploits the achievements of a few hundred citizens. Average individuality, over the great expanses of peasant and petty-bourgeois Russia, could scarcely leave its mark in anything which could compete for attractiveness, efficiency, or mere duration with the forms imposed by Tsarist power, by the Church and the wealthier nobles, and by the Russian capitalist in his last decades. These more striking older forms are now so often refurbished and assimilated into the Soviet picture that today the contrast between old and new can readily appear to be the contrast between stumbling individuality and the victories of central power.

It is a mistake, however, to imagine that Russians are continually making comparisons between 'the old' and 'the new' in the sense of pre- and post-revolutionary. What is visible all the time, what they are used to, is still largely the old, but its political implications have for many years been shrinking out of mind. Thirty years after 1917 it took a politically conscious foreigner to notice the fading advertisement for someone's coffee still high up in a traditional shopping street, or the red metal triangle of a pre-revolutionary beer still flapping on a house-end. Such rare details have lost significance. And if the domes of some old church of the Transfiguration or St Nicholas the Miracle-Worker still block the end of the avenue, probably not one in a thousand Russian unbelievers would today feel them a symbol which should be swept away. The contrast of pre- and post-1917 has mostly been merged into another contrast which is more living—what might be called the contrast between peasant and town standards, with the admission that the towns must still often rank as more than half peasant. It is a difference to be felt as one does the weekly shopping, between the modern stores and the traditional peasant market. The produce of the peasants' personal plots and animals is still a very great standby, and in times of shortage indeed a lifeline. In the cities there may be permanent market stalls set up by Soviet administration, but in hundreds of towns and villages the market spreads along the ground in the old way. Carrots, tomatoes, cabbages, and potatoes lie in the dust, chickens apparently lifeless are tied by the legs for you to prod, a kerchiefed woman offers you fried potatoes and Russian pancakes from a fire built among a few stones, while another will pour you milk from a vodka bottle, or vodka of a pale and cloudy yellow, home-distilled, from a battered kettle. A village grannie, failing to sell you her little porker, will kiss it on the nose to show her affection, and wandering among the knots of peasants is an office worker in a black suit, hoping to dispose of a dog-eared briefcase.

Prices in these markets are ruled by the laws of supply and demand. In wartime one could pay half an average weekly wage for a single apple, while in times of plenty the peasants must sell their spotty fruit for less than what is asked in the shops, not because they are regulated by any official tariff, but because no one will offer more. At the country stations, where an improvised market always gathers, fantastic prices may be asked of travellers, only to fall by a half as the train moves off.

It is all fascinating to the foreigner trying to sniff out 'Russian life', but to the townee Russian it is the shabby side of the familiar. It does not compare with the terrazzo floors and neat glass compartments of the new shops, where goods may be dear but their quality and price are more dependable. The best shops of Moscow, Leningrad, Kiev, and other cities may have several hundred kinds of sausage and cooked meats and smoked fish, even bread of a hundred kinds—poppyseed rolls, grey Minsk *pistolets*, puffwhite twistbreads, bread of every colour and texture from tasteless white to the meaty 'black' which can make a meal in itself without butter. There may be exotic foods from the South—grapes and tiny mandarines flown from the other side of the Caucasus, pistachios, huge 'saffron' apples from Turkestan, and sometimes imported pineapples and bananas for those who dare to try such fruits. And at last today there are clothing shops—not only in the centre of Moscow—which offer some variety of size, style, and design.

The contrasts which Russians notice, rather than those of pre- and post-Soviet régime, are the spectacular changes between this year and last year, two years, five years ago: a towering white block where there was a cluster of noisome shacks, a beautiful green train where there was only a service of battered box-cars, an array of gloves, socks, or aluminium pans where last year there were only a couple of sizes to be had. It does not matter that the new blocks, the new trains, and the new counters are packed to suffocation from the first day with people whose winter overcoats give off faint clouds of dust as they heave against each other. Anyone born as late as seven or eight years after the Revolution is old enough to have experienced two waves of this kind of expansion—from 1933 or so to 1941, and again in the 1950's. One of my earliest impressions of Moscow, in 1934, was of this kind of delight; during a three weeks' stay, my friends pointed out, I was privileged to see the opening of the first pâtisserie since the NEP period—a marble-countered place where you ate standing up as in France—and the appearance of two kinds of paper which had been absolutely non-existent. They were equally inadequate for their purpose, the writing paper of a hard chaffy surface almost too coarse to be used, and the toilet-paper soft to the point of disintegration, but at least they had, in form, arrived. Today, when the shops are packed with people buying, for instance, ten pounds of assorted soap or three dozen of matches at a time, everyone still says supplies, except of food, are short. But the quantities which you can already take home are such a compensation for the steaming tenement life and regulations, and the wearing out of energies in achieving the simplest repairs, that they generate an enthusiasm which easily infects the foreign visitor.

The Russian town scene is today an index, among other things, of the driving-power which the Soviet Government, in despite of all repressions, has been able to generate in its subjects, and it is a measure, too, of the belief and trust in the future which has superseded so much of the old hopelessness and lethargy. The attraction of the expanding urban life is such that the Government has long ago prevented peasants, in general, from taking town jobs except through official channels, though a good many still seem to get themselves recruited unofficially. One may hear townspeople speak of what is 'peasant' as *ipso facto* dirty and to be swept away in due course, like the ikons which, for years after the Revolution, used to sit at every street corner, slobbered and dripping with hearty moujik kisses. Under the latest reforms peasants are a great deal better off than they used to be, and some town workers consider them 'privileged', yet they are still coarsely dressed, are short of public services and entertainment, and have a much slenderer assortment of goods on the boards of the village co-op. than they can see in the city stores.

Some townspeople have been heard to speak of 'common people who live like animals'. Yet these are only the crude and brash among the town-dwellers, the newly-urbanized, who have kept a peasant coarseness and lost the peasant sense of brother-hood. The fact is that the countryside, for nearly all Russian townspeople, is at most only one generation away. It is where parents or uncles and aunts live, to visit whom is often the only chance of a holiday. The contrast between the material standards of town and peasant is new and striking, but there is still a great continuity between town and country, an inheritance of social ways and upbringing which is powerful in spite of being often unrealized or even superficially rejected by the new generation in town.

Understandably there is also a newer and more conscious kind of link becoming felt—a sense of the country as a green echo in the middle distance, such as grew up early in our own Industrial Revolution. Industrial Russia is sufficiently established already to feel the need of a green echo; for the more sophisticated or sensitive the city already transforms the country into what one might call a necessary poetic opposite. To have peasant roots may recall the bad old days of bugs and illiteracy, of uncertain feeding and cramped living, of the unlighted life in the 'bears' corner', but they can also be the good old days; they are the link with the father-figure who sings old folk-songs and raises honey; they are part of the national character.

The country background, of course, is not the same as the English country background, and the relationship is by no means the same. Russia used to breed, in a small class, a country-gentleman attitude which had some resemblance to its English counterpart, but this could not filter down through Russian society as it has filtered in England from grand estates to young men with sports cars living in bedsitters, or ladies who maintain a proprietorial relationship to their village neighbours on an income of six pounds a week. In Russia it certainly did not breed the admiration for the life of a country gentleman which is so embedded in English life. If one of the intelligentsia today affects a country manner, it is probably a projection of his virility—to create the impression that he is a peasant or a hunter, albeit a gifted one, temporarily camping out in the society of Moscow or

Leningrad. Only perhaps at the very top, among the six-figure incomes of such as the late Alexei Tolstoy, there may be some lavishness of countryhouse life which derives, though much watered down, from the old noble tradition. Fundamentally the background is not that of a feudal or aristocratic countryside. It is first the village, with its simple communal ways and supplies of fresh food in summer, and then the space and the wild—the wild where a man can hunt. I have seen a red fox shot on a Sunday at Moscow's equivalent of Hampton Court, and any man who can get a gun and cartridges will find wild duck, black-cock, and partridge if he ventures only a little farther, while bears, wolves, and lynxes are said still to haunt forests as near to Moscow as Bedfordshire is to London.

Electric lamps and television sets are beginning to appear in the countryside, but their owners still live in *izbas*, and the Russian countryside is still the soil in which Russian society and Russian character have grown. One can get to know the Russian people in the squalid back-streets of their towns, but it is easier, if only one has the opportunity, to get to know them in the country, where new values and new objects do not jostle so thickly; one can more easily see what kind of people they are who have taken up with new values and new objects—or been taken up by them—and how they are different from what Englishmen or Americans or Frenchmen might be in similar conditions.

Only one must not judge the peasants too much, as one would judge in Western Europe, by what they make of their surroundings. If there is little sweetness in huts or gardens, the sweetness is there in the people—in the warm hospitality, in the good nature of the peasant crowds however thick they throng in trains or markets, in the old country nannies who attach themselves to hundreds of modest city families as well as privileged ones, in the beautiful courtesy of so many of the old. (The most distinguished of all the courteous old peasants I met had no better home in wartime than a hole in the mud outskirts of Kuibyshev.)

And if the sweetness is to be seen in human relationships rather than in the work of men's hands, then it seems to me that, with every material shortage and hardship allowed for, the bias must be deeply significant of something in the Russian character. External appearances in Russia are far less informative than in the West. The endless plantations of *izbas* have their history indeed, but it is trampled in the ashes of a hundred fires. In Russia the history, even more than in other countries, is enshrined in the people.

Zagorsk, Cathedral of the Assumption, and a chapel of the late
eighteenth century

The fir forest is tallest in the north

On feast days—here an election day—three horses can sometimes still be harnessed to make the traditional *troika*

Spring begins on Nikitsky Boulevard, Moscow

The Volga in Central Russia, near Ples

Cleaning the church at Brest-Litovsk, the women chant portions of the service

Saratov, in south-east Russia, typical urban architecture of the nineteenth century

Apartment blocks in the new south-western suburb of Moscow, 1959

A village of *izbas*—larger and closer together than usual

A reconstructed village in the south

A room in a new Moscow flat, 1959

The centre of the largest Government Universal Store ('G.U.M.') in Moscow

4

Being a Russian

THE FIRST Russians I ever knew were refugees from the Bolshevik Revolution living in South Kensington. The Diaghilev Ballet was in its heyday, I was very young, and I not unnaturally expected that life among Russians—even refugee Russians—would have some exotic quality, some reflection of the colour and sparkle of such a scene as the opening of *Petrouchka*. In this expectation I was disappointed, as many have been before me. I found myself in a scene where costumes and *décor*, so to speak, were vague and of small account, except on a few very formal occasions; almost everything significant seemed to be concentrated in the *dramatis personae*. I found myself received into a *milieu* where personal relationships and personal expression had an importance, a development, a naturalness and 'sincerity', as I called it, such as I had never imagined.

In this company self-assurance was apparently little valued, as in some Western circles, for its own sake, without evaluation of the self which is exhibiting assurance or the occasion when assurance is being shown. There was a certain formality in this society of formerly privileged persons, but the essential element in *savoir-faire* appeared for them to be less the conformity to a code than a fundamental naturalness of behaviour, a fundamental loyalty to one's own feelings. If you didn't like a painting which they showed you, it was gauche to pretend an enthusiasm which you could not feel; they seemed able to see through any protestations, and they would let you know that they saw through them and yet manage not to give offence. If you felt bored or tired or sad in Russian company it was a solecism not to admit it if asked.

When a Russian inquires of you—'Vam skutchno?' ('Are you fed up, bored?')—the question is not to be felt as somewhat embarrassing, requiring that you should defend yourself and protest that you are, on the contrary, enjoying his company, or the journey, or the play. It is a sympathetic enquiry, of the same order as 'Don't you feel well?' There are special words in Russian for the two kinds of sympathy—the receptive and the outgoing. Russians delight in people who are both *chutky* (sensitive in appreciating other people's moods and situations) and *otzyvchivy* (full of sympathetic response).

The quality which enchanted me in my Russian acquaintances was not, I discovered, merely the outpouring of generous and mature natures for the benefit of a diffident young Englishman; it was shown still more in the way that they behaved to each other. Neither was it a quality which had become over-developed among refugees who, having lost most of their possessions, had little but personal relationships with which to maintain their sense of continuity. The same naturalness of behaviour, the same respect for and expression of genuine personal feeling seemed to me characteristic when I eventually visited Russia. It is this, in fact, which has always impressed foreigners who have come to know Russians well, whether in their own country or in exile. Even Russians who have no dealings with foreigners are themselves aware of the quality; they are proud of what they call their 'broad', 'capacious' (*shiroky*) nature.

However, my dominant impression of the people, on first going into Russia, was of quite another character. A sea of rather grey-blond faces for the most part, they were many of them unfamiliar types in feature—that is, those who were Russian, and leaving aside the occasional Mongol or sallow hook-nosed Georgian or Armenian. There were round, potato-like peasant faces of the kind later typified for the West by Marshal Timoshenko. There were flattish faces with concave noses, cheeks scarred and flattened by frostbite, pale faces with pale blue eyes bored deep in the head and a scowl between. They had little to eat in those days, and some faces were ravaged by poor feeding, a few even bleeding from scurvy. Almost all the women were short and stocky, but there were some large burly men built like Chaliapin, and now and then a tall handsome Scandinavian-looking young man or girl. There were open-faced blondes of the type that goes with braided hair, though too slight to be Brünn-hildes, and these occasionally had eyes so burning blue that one wondered if such unfathomable lakes of candour could reflect anything at all. There were pale, steely, Molotov-like intellectuals, and once or twice the very goatee and pince-nez of a Tchehov. But quite half of them were the same sort of miscellaneous brownish types as myself and millions more of Europe's city-dwellers. If one overlooked the washed-out, khaki-greyish clothes and the women's neglected hair, the crowds could have passed super-ficially as English, French, Swiss, German, Dutch, Swedes. . . . They could pass, that is, as to features and colouring. But expres-sion was another matter. For whether Nordic, 'peasant', or non-descript, almost all these Russian faces had one thing in common. They were peculiarly expressionless and detached; they seemed neither very self-aware nor aware of much outside themselves.

There was no challenge in people's eyes as they looked at each other in passing; in fact they looked at each other but little. They bumped into one another without apology and apparently without offence. If a man changed direction abruptly in the crowd, he never looked behind to see if he were cutting off some-one else, nor did the cut-off ones seem to mind. They must all feel themselves, I thought, to be members of one vast incon-sequent family. Presently I was able to observe that instructive Russian trait, the inability to form a queue. And the significant aspect of this seemed to me not so much the formlessness which makes Russians unable to queue without being made to, as the fact that their unregulated ways so rarely cause bad feeling. In the Moscow Metro, for instance, the doors open to the same width as in the underground trains of other countries; if two or three persons were to step in neatly abreast, the crowd would soon be absorbed. But this, presumably, would be too great a reversal of Russian habit. A great hemisphere of passengers hurls itself against the doors, and of the eight or nine persons jammed in the opening, perhaps one is at first shot into the carriage, leaving the glove of his rearmost hand nipped in the throng. As the jam follows him, hats are stripped off heads, buttons ripped off coats, and enormous officers wearing half a hundredweight of clothing are tossed about like logs in a swell. They grin and do not mind. Hardly anyone minds. The delay is stupid, but eventually the carriage is filled. And the secret of it all seems to be that the crowd pushes, but no one person pushes, so that there is no one to get angry with. Unless perhaps it is a foreigner like myself, who was made to feel mortally ashamed once when I lost my temper and lashed out back, sides, and front at my neighbours to get some breathing-space. 'To have to travel with such people!' they said with indignant scorn.

The same community feeling is seen even when two Russians have a row. It will scarcely be over such a trifle as a compressed stomach in the Metro—more likely the climax of repeated frustrations over the kitchen or lavatory which is shared, in so many Russian apartments, by five or six families. The two parties do not roar at each other; they rather whine or wheedle, as if each trying to persuade the other that he must, in all good sense and feeling, admit that right is not on his side. The neighbours or passers-by take a hand in endeavouring to convert one or both to a socially acceptable view of the situation. A quarrel in public is not quite the thing; it is described by the foreign word *skandal*. And a fight between Russians is still more rare, indeed almost unheard of between men who have not been drinking. When they do fight it is a chaos of pushing and hauling, grabbing with one hand and punching with the other, and breaking off at intervals to glare as though saying, not 'Are you beaten yet?' but 'Are you going to agree, damn you?' Not the last word but the agreement is what seems to count, and a fight may end with brotherly arms around necks and the sharing a bottle of vodka.

One soon learns how frequent theft can be in Russia (it seems diminished only now that the supply of consumer goods is at last so much increased); there can be burglary, robbery with violence, and in some city districts a good deal of unpleasant hooliganism, yet for the most part one comes to feel safe among Russian people. Strange they may be, cut off if one does not know the language, but there is never the fear that an accidental contretemps may break out into hysteria as can happen in Germany. Still less is there the Mediterranean safety-valve of violently-expressed feelings, where stages and limits are observed as though in an art form. Yet in spite of their generally unexcited exterior the Russian people do not give the impression of being an inhibited race.

It is twenty-six years since I first visited Russia, but the dominant characteristics of the people still seem to me the same as they did then—the strong, largely unconscious sense of community, and the naturalness and truth-to-feeling of individual behaviour. These are the two poles to which, I believe, most of the features peculiar to Russian behaviour can be related. At least, most of the traits which strike an Englishman as strange can be explained by reference to these two poles, but the explanations are by no means easy. For the Russian sense of community is not the same as either the sense of fellowship or the sense of nationhood in countries further west. And the very spontaneity of Russians can make them harder to interpret, for those who were brought up in traditions of greater discipline. Still more difficult to grasp is the interrelationship between the apparently free behaviour of the individual and his sense of the Russian community. For if every Russian acts as he feels, is it only by totalitarian discipline that anything can get done? Or on the other hand, if the sense of belonging to the Russian family is so strong, how can a Russian act freely as an individual? And how is it possible for the liberal give-and-take of his personal contacts to extend outside the family to a foreigner?

The answers to these questions are not simple, and my attempts to supply them will spread from this chapter to the next, and into several other chapters of this book.

To bridge the contrast between one's impression of individual Russians and one's impression of the mass is a sort of *pons asinorum* in understanding Russia, which it is no easy task to cross. Contacts were fairly free in 1934, when I first visited Russia, but I had never felt so much an outsider in any of the dozen other countries I had visited. If I merely asked the way in Leningrad people would not reply, or would call out 'Shan't say!' (though as my Russian grew more idiomatic I found that this may also mean 'Can't say'). There was none of the German gushing over a foreigner nor the embarrassing Italian desire to help. Nor was I just a forbidden person, marked off by my obvious foreign clothes. The tram conductor and the shop assistant were as offhand to their fellow Russians as they were to me, and the Russians in the street were as offhand to each other.

It might be asked if these were not simply the reactions of a populace cowed by dictatorship. Yet one has only to visit Soviet Georgia or Soviet Armenia to find races living under the same government but far more demonstrative, flamboyant, and even aggressive in behaviour. The apparent lack of demonstrativeness must seem to be more a Russian than a Soviet characteristic.

Within twenty-four hours of arriving in Leningrad, however, I had made my first Russian acquaintance. We met in one of the city's rare cafés, a bare, drab, flyblown establishment fit for a scene in *Crime and Punishment*, where I was sitting with another English tourist who wanted to draw Russian types. She began surreptitiously enough with an old peasant at the other end of our scrubbed yellow table, but when he discovered what was happening he objected loudly to being sketched as he drank his tea in the old Russian way, holding the sugar in pursed lips and sucking the tea out of his saucer through the sugar. It wasn't right to come to a tea place and draw people, he protested. At this the whole café burst out—it must be said they were drinking their own tea out of the glass—in defence of the foreigner, and the old uncle was so badgered to say where the harm was in sketching that he went out in a huff. The artist was invited to draw anyone she pleased, but her nerve was shaken and she retired to her hotel. The café relapsed into quiet, and I thought a word of acknowledgment was due to a young man who had more or less led the movement in our defence. To my surprise he proposed a stroll together if I had nothing better to do, and we went out into the Nevsky Prospekt. He was insistent that we should not have formed a bad impression of Russian manners from the old peasant, who had in fact meant no harm, and then I was asked to talk of Shakespeare, for the young man was himself a small-part actor beginning to specialize in comedy. He was short, long-nosed, quite unactorlike, and his name was Yefim. I had not got over my surprise at this introduction to Russian life when I was invited to praise the paintings of William Blake, but my Russian was not at that time equal to discussing them as my new friend would have wished. We arranged to meet again next day, and went by bus to the gardens at the mouth of the Neva, where I was to be shown the Strelka, the classic promenade at the very edge of Leningrad, where one looks out over the Gulf of Finland. But Yefim had never been to the Strelka himself, and it was strangely difficult to find. He asked the way of one person after another and met with quite half a dozen of the surly or offhand replies to which I had grown accustomed, until a naval officer at length had the politeness to tell us the way. Yefim took all this behaviour as a matter of course, and in spite of his subtlety about Blake, it seemed he was not the person to solve the problem of the Russian crowd for me.

I made other acquaintances—a lecturer in an art gallery, and a young man at the theatre who opened conversation with the magic words 'Vam skutchno?' because I was yawning my head off at a Meyerhold production which I could not follow. Both of these wanted to talk about literature to the countryman of Shakespeare, Shaw, and Byron, but they could not explain their own countrymen to me. I compared notes with other visitors and our impressions coincided; most of us had made a contact or two which had surprised us into delight, but we were baffled by the contrast between these and the behaviour of the casual crowd. It was only much later that I came across a clue, in conversation with a woman who had worked at one time for Intourist, the State organization which handles foreign tourists. She was telling me as much about her training as she thought fit for me to hear: 'We noticed', she said, 'that English people and all foreigners smile very much. It is a custom, no? When we Russians meet a new person we do not smile unless, of course, we think we like the person at once. It is not necessary to smile unless we feel like it. So among the guides we had a saying—"Remember, many smiles!"'

So that was the key to the dull expressions of the shuffling crowds. The offhandedness was not, after all, the Russian community warding off the foreigner, but the Russian individual, weary, unused to city habits, drowning in a sea of strangers, who was unable to raise interest in a casual enquiry and who had not yet acquired the pleasing if hollow urbanity of the city-dweller in some other countries. He was being true to himself in his offhand or lifeless way, as true to himself as the most exhilarating of our new acquaintances. I now understood why there was among Russians so little tossing of greetings or playing ball with banal remarks to warm up good fellowship. If good fellowship was not felt on both sides at a particular moment, what was the good of trying to warm it up? Faces would light up when there was sufficient reason, and not merely for the small change of personal intercourse. The same key seemed to explain the difficulty I had found about staring. A foreigner naturally stares, and I could never repress also the kind of stare which tries to read a man's story from a heavy brow, a listless coat collar, a despairing or a lively tread. The limit of embarrassment, I found, was reached much sooner in Russia than in England, though no one actually challenged my lack of manners. A Frenchman, if he thinks you are staring too hard, fights back at least with his eyes, an Englishman tries to make out he hasn't noticed, but a Russian assumes you want something—probably you want to start a conversation. (You can, of course, and do start conversations in Russia, on holiday, in restaurants, in trains and trams, and Russians, except for a few bores, open with a rather charming diffidence, implying that they propose contact if you also care to make it.) The Russian is the unselfconscious man, living in a society of unselfconscious men, and if you stare into his detachment he presumes you have a reason. There is nothing mystic about this detachment in the average Russian. It is the composure of a man whose behaviour was very little fussed over when he was a child, and who is at home among his fellows who were equally unfussed over. No one expects another to assert himself merely for the sake of establishing his identity, and Russians are ill at ease with people brought up in a convention of self-assertion.

One may observe the contrast of this Russian composure without leaving England, among the small groups of expatriate Russians whose expressions, even in the younger generation, can often appear so dull and amorphous in repose, and yet light up into such unexpected and generous humanity when they begin to talk. For several years, when I travelled daily by an underground line which passes near the Soviet Embassy in London, I was repeatedly surprised to hear Russian spoken by passengers whom I would have taken to be English. I recognized some Russians because they had features which are rarely seen outside their own country, and others—the newly-arrived, no doubt—were distinguishable by their coarse and poorly designed clothes. But I continued to lose bets with myself about others, with their frequently English or Nordic features and their good English suits, until I fastened upon their more-than-English withdrawal into inner calm, their lack of expression when silent or exchanging the casual phrase, their more-than-English liveliness when they engaged in conversation, and the enquiring response in their eyes if they intercepted my stare.

Once a foreigner has grasped something of the Russian feeling of composure among one's fellows, he will begin to feel at home in Russia too. He will understand how it is that he can walk into one Russian village and be ignored, how in another he may be overwhelmed with hospitality, and how he can knock at almost any hut in any village with the certainty of not being refused a glass of tea. The only time I ever found a bare little *chainaya*, or tea house, open in a Russian village, I was referred to 'any hut' for my tea. The *chainaya* was serving vodka in little red flower-pots, but a glass of tea was the business of common hospitality. In spite of all the savage interference of Soviet collectivization one can still feel, as the classic authority Sir Donald Mackenzie Wallace found in the 1870's, that 'no class of men in the world are more good-natured and pacific than the Russian peasantry'. And in spite of occasional peasant violence, and much peasant artfulness in bargaining, that is still what one's town friends in Soviet Russia expect to feel. Some of the old habits have weakened under the stress of life in cities, but most of the townspeople whom I knew seemed to feel themselves fundamentally still part of the ancient community.

It is into this good-natured community that the ordinary Russian invites you when he takes a liking to you. For although he is full of curiosity about foreigners, and always ready to hear of something new, when he takes you to his bosom he is delighted most at finding that you also, the outsider, are as he puts it 'ours' (*nash*). That *nash* is a word of great potency. It is applied to the Russian landscape, to Lenin, to vodka, to Russian bread, to a good friend, to the Soviet Army. I have heard it applied to Tchehov, and to new power lines across the steppe, and I have heard it used with sad and shocked surprise about a trainload of forced labour prisoners going to work behind the lines in time of war.

The family feeling among Russians is fortified by the very names by which they call each other. Almost everyone is addressed by his or her Christian name and father's Christian name, the surname being kept for formal use. Most Russians, in fact, had no surnames until comparatively recent times; they were called 'the Alexanders' Michael' (Mikhail Alexandrov) or 'the Anthonys' Vera' (Vera Antonina), and when Michael married Vera their son Paul would be 'the Michaels' Paul' (Pavel Mikhailov), adopting the father's Christian name just as Icelanders (who have no surnames) do to this day. Only after the liberation of the serfs did all these names in -*ov* and -*in* become surnames, leaving names in -*vitch* and -*ovna* (which were formerly much higher in status) as middle names meaning 'son of' and 'daughter of', as now. So that today an ordinary name such as Alexander Mikhailovitch

Stolyarov might be rendered in English by something like the archaic flavour of 'the Carpenters' Alexander, Michael's son', but in Russian this is not felt to be archaic or colloquial. Stolyarov ('of the Carpenters') is the man's name on his identity papers, and there are occasions, under Soviet administration, when he is addressed as 'Comrade Stolyarov'. But to people with whom he has the slightest acquaintance he is Alexander Mikhailovitch (or rather Mikhail'itch), whether he is among friends or relations or workmates, whether he is the lowest grade of worker being addressed by the works manager or the manager being addressed by the lowest grade of worker, whether he is a student being addressed by a professor or a professor being addressed by a student, even on such a formal occasion as the public celebration of the professor's eightieth birthday. In the old days serfs used such titles as *barin* or *gospodin* to those above them, but they called their own master, or any master whom they personally knew, by his Christian name and patronymic. And in Soviet times Khrushchev can be both Comrade Khrushchev and Nikita Sergeyevitch.

When two Russians make temporary acquaintance, it is not long before one of them will excuse himself and ask for the other's *imya* and *otchestvo*—his Christian name and father's Christian name. These exchanged, the conversation proceeds upon a proper footing, in an atmosphere perhaps a shade warmer than the atmosphere of 'Mr Carpenter' and 'Mr Smith', but less intimate than where Christian names alone are used. Russians treat their foreign acquaintances in the same way, even though their names may fit clumsily into the language. My own name being the same as my father's, I became 'Rait Raitovitch'. A combination such as 'Gladys Stanleyovna' may look ridiculous, but if Russians take a liking to Gladys, daughter of Stanley, they are offended if she will not accept this version of her name; it is the token of her admission into the family.

First names in Russia are nearly all taken from the limited traditional stock of Ivan, Nikolai, Peter, Paul, Michael, Igor, Anton, Sergei, Ilya (Elias), etc., and a similarly restricted list for women. They are almost all biblical or saints' names—I came across an Athanasius and an Arsène—and the Bolshevik régime has made very little difference to them, though it would be wrong to take this as a sign of the continuing power of the Russian Church. The Revolution produced a few new names, of which the only one now much favoured is Oktyabrina (from the October Revolution), and that rather because it makes a pretty name for a girl than for political reasons. There has been no other impulse to produce fresh names, and Russians would not think it quite human to start naming their children by the Russian equivalents of Dawn or Fern or Dale. So that living in a land of Alexander Mikhail'itches, Mikhail Alexandr'itches, Mikhail Mikhail'itches, Alexander Alexandr'itches and so forth is rather like the Russian landscape—repetitive but comfortingly familiar to those brought up in it. Differences of rank and position are thus to some extent absorbed into the feeling of a common stock.

It is vast and somewhat vague, the common stock of which the Russian feels himself to be a member. Only in wartime does it harden into something like nationhood in face of an aggressor. The feeling of being Russian is less definite than the gnawing sense of nationality in peoples like the Poles or the Irish who have suffered long periods of foreign rule; but neither is it the mere assumption that any other Russian is probably all right, while foreigners are peculiar. It is rather the feeling of a community of all warmhearted and reasonable men—the Russians, of course, having a greater share than other nations of the right sort of heart and the right sort of reason. But while most foreign states, as states, are believed to have intended and to intend little good to Russia, there is felt to be room inside the Russian community for numbers of individual foreigners. A striking story in this connection is told by F. Beck and W. Godin in their account of their experiences as political prisoners, *Russian Purge*:

In each cell a 'charity-committee' was elected, whose task it was to provide for those who had no money to spend. A contribution of from 10 per cent to 20 per cent of what they bought was levied on the more prosperous inmates.

This share-out was normally carried out with complete fairness, and all the prisoners in every cell were normally regarded as equals. In one cell there was a senior party official, a member of the Central Committee, a typical orthodox representative of the party line. One of his cell-mates was an extremely rare specimen, an obviously genuine spy, who had crossed the border from Poland and admitted he was under orders from the Polish Government. The senior party official raised the question whether a genuine enemy of the Soviet Union should take part in the share-out or not. The question was put to the vote, and it was decided by a large majority that the man should have the same share as the rest.

The Russian community is not rigid; it never acquired enough formal institutions or traditional objects to be that. In the old village quite a number of the men at any one time were on the move, tramping to look for a change of work or just for the sake of tramping. These wanderers were not outcasts. If they went to live in towns, even if they became well-off, they kept the ties with their village. The enterprise of the individual did not separate him from his fellows, and the Russian community still has this character of appearing part of the natural order, more ancient than those conscious and sophisticated communities (as among colonial settlers) which were created and maintained by individuals-in-their-own-right for their common advantage and enjoyment. Even when the Russian community honours one of its members it does not set him apart; when your health is being drunk in Russia you must rise and drink with the company. If you are being given an ovation you join in the applause and clap back, as I have seen no less a person than Stalin doing from his box at the opera. It is all as though the simple Russian felt himself to be less sharply marked off from the body of his fellows than the average Westerner does.

What are the roots of the Russian community feeling? It is a commonplace to suggest how much it must derive from the Orthodox Church—that ancient loosely organized Church or association of Churches, which is proud of having evolved so little from the state of the early Christian communities. The sense of a special destiny for Russians within the general brotherhood of man, still so potent in the USSR, is certainly due originally to the Russian Church. An essential condition of blessedness, in the Orthodox view, has always consisted in the being gathered together; Catholics by their authoritarianism and Protestants by their individualism are thought to have lost this pristine state.

A cathedral in Russian is not named after the bishop's chair or *cathedra*; it is called *sobor*, a word which in the first place means 'gathering'. And at a Russian church service one does indeed feel oneself a member of an informal, comfortable gathering. Warmer and livelier than the Quaker experience of being 'in meeting', participation in a Russian service lacks the Quaker individualism entirely, but it is more passive than the feeling in an Anglican church, since Russian congregations do not join in the singing, use no books, and never sit down. Yet the Russian congregation, even though walking about sometimes or exchanging remarks during the service, helps to create that feeling of *sobornost* or 'congregationalness' which is regarded as so blest. To experience profoundly this feeling of fellowship with even the dirtiest and most lowly one must attend one of the Easter Eve services which have so often been described in Russian novels. All quarrels are to be forgiven, all men truly made brethren, at this great ceremony, and the effects of this sublime joining together are supposed to last the whole of the subsequent year. Today, when few Russians attend church regularly, enormous numbers still join in the Easter service.

Standing shoulder to shoulder in the dingy, fearsomely packed cathedral, one finds no air but the vapour of sweat and already much-spent breath, while from the ceiling fifty feet above great drops of tepid condensation splash upon the immovable mass of worshippers. Byzantine saints, painted in tiers round the walls, peer through the wreaths of incense; the unseen choir, reinforced by a few opera singers, chants with scarcely a pause, unaccompanied as always in Orthodox services; and the only light, apart from the candles held by every member of the congregation, is concentrated far off on the gold brocades of the priests and the gilded gates of the sanctuary. One is exhausted by standing for three or four hours with no possibility of relief, yet in this state of suffocation, or outside in the even larger crowd, lit by hundreds of little candles, exchanging Easter greetings with every neighbour, listening to those who can intone fragments of the service, passing greasy notes over twenty yards of heads to pay for candles, and passing candles back, one feels for the time being a member of a simple, almost childlike community which does not let go of its everyday humanity while it waits for a revelation to descend. It is impossible for all the worshippers to find room in the cathedral, but those outside may share perhaps more dramatically in the highest moment of the service. For at midnight the priests march in procession round the outside of the building until they stop before its doors, which had been closed to symbolize the mouth of the Tomb. Suddenly the doors are opened, and in a burst of gold and candlelight and a climax of singing the procession enters the cathedral to chant the hymns of Easter morning. The stone has been rolled away and the faithful have seen—the truly pious say they have 'experienced'—the Resurrection once more. It is after this, for the whole of Easter week, that people exchange with each other and with the priests the Easter kiss and Easter greeting—'Christ is risen!': 'He is risen indeed!' It is spoken with a kind of joyous solemnity. When you first naïvely venture the greeting yourself to religious-minded Russians you feel that a whole window has opened upon the Russian world; they pause to impress you with the solemnity of the moment, and reply as though you had made them some declaration of affection. The crowd at an Easter service in modern Russia does not consist entirely of convinced believers, any more than the crowd at an English Christmas service, but near-believers would rather avoid the greeting than debase it to the level of a mere bright friendliness. And at the Easter service, whether moved by nostalgia for something which they cannot recapture, or by the desire to participate in a communal ceremony, or by the stirring of a spring rite in the April air—if they can no longer share in the repetition of the very Resurrection, if the revelation for them does not descend, yet at least the near-believers will have been able to enter into the feeling of brotherhood and congregation.

Yet powerful though the Orthodox Church has been in maintaining and to some extent in breeding the Russian community feeling, the Church alone cannot be responsible for it, or one would find a similar feeling carried over into daily life in every Orthodox country, even in individualistic Greece. There is a basic difference, however, between the life led by Russians over many centuries and the life led by Greeks or, for that matter, by most other European peoples. For while the Greeks, even under the Turkish domination, mostly led the life of independent peasants, few Russians were ever independent peasants at all, whether during or after the period of serfdom. The exceptions have been either on that 'frontier' which was always being pushed further south and east, or during the last years before the Revolution, when land reform began to encourage a small class who might have developed into a vigorous individual peasantry. Apart from these exceptions the Russian peasants, until the collectivization of 1930, lived and worked in village communities under the traditional organization of the Mir. The Mir held the land and distributed it, good and bad, in a patchwork intended to be as equitable as possible between families. The Mir fixed the times of ploughing, sowing, haymaking, and harvest. The Mir disciplined individuals when necessary, and however much dispute and bad feeling there might be between individuals and families, no one rebelled against the authority of the Mir.

The Mir was neither a person nor a committee, neither an authority imposed from above nor a representative of any higher authority. Its origins are too obscure for historians to be able to agree whether, or how, the Mir arose from the patriarchal 'great family' system which preceded it, but in all the records it appears to be regarded by the peasants as part of their natural state. *Mir* is a word which has no plural form; it is the same word, historically, as the word for 'world', and the Mir was the peasants' world. 'The Mir cannot be judged', they said; 'Throw all upon the Mir, it will bear all.'

The Mir was the village assembly, but it would scarcely be accurate to call it anything so self-conscious as the political institution of the village; it was rather the village operating in its political aspect. Its meetings usually began, we are told, as informal knots of men standing in an open space chatting, and eventually coalescing into a single group discussing a single topic. In this group the elected Elder, or *Starosta*, did not stand out until it was necessary for him to take the opinion of the meeting. Disputes, it appeared, would generally subside into a common recognition that one decision rather than another was equitable or inevitable. Sometimes the Elder was obliged to count heads, and in such cases the minority always accepted the majority verdict. Although the Mir was taken so much for granted no one, it is reported, was anxious to be chosen as Elder or for any other office, but once chosen he would carry out his functions and no one would dispute his authority. The Mir must have been for the individual a way of vesting the responsibility for decisions—especially awkward decisions—outside himself, and at the same time of feeling that he was part of the process of deciding. In 1888 L. Tikhomirov wrote (in *Russia, Political and Social*):

The Great Russian cannot imagine a life outside his society, outside the Mir. The Ukrainian on the other hand sometimes says, 'What belongs to all belongs to the devil'. The Great Russian says: 'The Mir is a fine fellow, I will not desert the Mir. Even death is beautiful in common.'

To betray the commune, says this author, was for the Great Russian the greatest possible, the one unpardonable sin.

The Ukrainian reaches the idea of public welfare by taking as his starting-point the exigencies of his individual rights . . . he finds great difficulty in giving up his individual independence, even if the sacrifice is for the commonweal . . . the Great Russian from the idea of public welfare deduces that of his rights.

Such was the society in which something like 80 per cent of the Russian people lived until many years after the Revolution. And although peasants now form slightly less than half the population, yet most Russians born earlier than say 1920, whether farm workers or town workers, must have been brought up in the atmosphere of the Mir, while persons under that age, if born in country districts, were born into communities where the old feeling is still strong. The collectivization of 1930–33 deported or killed off the independent peasants, it starved vast numbers of others by its naïve brutality and inefficiency, it converted the old patchwork of the Mir lands into lands which were held and farmed in common, and from these lands it demanded fixed returns of produce for the State, but it preserved the villages as basic units (now called 'collective farms') and it preserved the General Assembly of the Collective Farmers. The Assembly now had a Chairman, often imposed rather than elected, and he was armed with power which he was meant to use, but the Assembly still united the villagers, and not least in defence of the small private plots which remained to them. In 1951 a second collectivization concentrated the farms into multi-village units of twice the previous size. There was also an attempt to make the peasants leave their villages and concentrate in 'agro-towns', but it met with so much resistance that it had to be dropped. An inevitable result of so many years of interference has been to drive the country people more compactly together, in a reaction which anyone in town clothes can feel as he attempts to make contact with suspicious villagers. Under the Khrushchev reforms there have been further amalgamations of collective farms, but the regional machine-and-tractor stations have been dissolved and their equipment handed over to the farms, the peasants are at last getting a reasonable price for their deliveries to the state, their taxes are reduced, and each family retains as ever its private plot.

Before a Russian child could feel much of its status in the world of the Mir, however, it was being conditioned, like any other child, by the immemorial attitudes and methods of bringing up infants, and indeed it might be said that in speculating on the origins of the Russian character one should have fastened first on these.

One does not need any psychological training or bias to notice the importance of the traditional Russian attitude in bringing up young children. Even before one has been invited into a Russian family one is bound to see how tolerant and patient every Russian is with the young, whether they are his own offspring or not. Patience seems longer than in England, and when it is at last exhausted, a Russian almost never slaps or shakes a child. Corporal punishment in schools does not exist. Yet few Russian children seem spoilt—perhaps because they are all, or almost all, brought up in the same way, and perhaps also because Russians do not sentimentalize much over children; their attitude is a rather unusual blend of affection and detachment. Parents rarely seem to be over-possessive. Traditionally any Russian peasant mother might give suck to any other's child in the field if convenient, whereas among Polish peasants to do so brought 'bad luck'. In the villages Russian children have always been accustomed to a background of benevolence and help from every adult, and adoptions, we are told, are not difficult to arrange. Most Russian children are left to grow naturally into clean habits; if their knickers are wet they are not disciplined, and neither is any fuss made about regular feeding-times. At a maternity centre which I visited in Leningrad regular feeding and bowel habits were being recommended, according to the director, as part of the infant routine, but any number of such centres must have uphill work against the weight of Russian grandmothers and their traditions.

The exceptions, according to my observation, are of two kinds. Among the intelligentsia there are some families with more Western ideas of child training. A few of their young people grow up with a rather harassed and preoccupied expression which is unRussian, but they do not seem to develop the gnawing superego so familiar in Protestant countries. The other exceptions belong to the coddled minority, frequently complained of in the Soviet press, who grow up to be as egocentric, demanding, and lacking in self-discipline as coddled children are liable to do anywhere. For these families the traditional lack of discipline remains, but the old atmosphere is broken by the possessiveness of the parents. The number of such children is almost certainly increasing, owing to the improved material conditions of a small class, and the possibilities of isolation for more and more families in towns.

But for the great mass of Russian children, whether the mother goes out to work or not, the continuity of their little lives is centred largely on the grandmother. 'The babouchka,' said an ex-peasant to whom I owe much of my information, 'the babouchka is the key. If the parent is cross or uncomprehending it is the granny who comforts the child and explains to it why parents must sometimes be so. And especially it is the granny who tells the fairy stories.' The babouchka does not, however, dominate the household, or if in an individual case she does so, it is because she is a strongminded old lady and not as of right. She is the paternal grandmother (the maternal grandmother will usually stay with one of her own sons when she is widowed) and she does not detract from the paternal domination—it would sound too heavy nowadays to call it patriarchal—which is still characteristic of the Russian family. Thus even in an isolated town family (and in Russian housing conditions few families can be so isolated) the Russian child, though lacking the many grannies and aunts and uncles of the village, has at least one other adult than his parents to form a background of security.

Certainly if any class of Soviet citizens gives the impression of being happy, even in times of hardship, it is the young children. They are friendly without being bold, and they develop a pleasant, unselfconscious confidence. To all appearance they are not unduly burdened by their efforts to adjust themselves to their little society. 'Collective play' in Soviet schools today builds on, or intensifies, an old Russian habit. And as families grow up they very often stay together, even in the most up-to-date housing conditions, Mr Khrushchev's family being apparently an example.

I have not here described the influences which may have helped to form Russian 'character' (or more precisely Russian social attitudes and habits) for their own sake—for they deserve much more space—but so that they may help to describe, as much as to explain, the peculiarities which strike Westerners in Russians today.

The Russian, I suggest, growing up in self-confidence without much childhood discipline, a member of a secure, ancient, but loose community, not conditioned before his schooldays to any large number of habits, rituals, or taboos, displays that natural-ness which has so often enchanted foreigners, that 'sincerity' which I put in quotation marks at the beginning of this chapter. I distinguished the word in this way because it does not exactly describe—nor does any single English word describe—the funda-mental Russian quality of behaving according to one's feelings, and also because I wished to avoid the suggestion, so often attached to the word, that a person who is morally admirable in being sincere is likely to be morally admirable in other ways. The 'sincerity' of a shallow Russian character can be repulsive—the 'sincerity', for example, of the doglike creature called Foma, or Thomas, who used to haunt the foreign colony in Moscow. He was not the only one who hoped, in attaching himself to foreigners, to profit by a cake of soap, a pot of jam, or a cast-off shirt, nor could one grudge him these in war conditions. But one was also called on to endure the outpouring of his tenth-rate soul, to admire the shrewdness he showed in cultivating our acquain-tance, and to applaud his ingenuity in avoiding the call-up for timber-cutting. Yet this was his sincerity—the way he spoke his feelings and was true to them. He was as genuine in his way as our most delightful Russian friends were in theirs.

But if the Russian 'sincerity' means that one has to endure self-revelation from shallow souls, it means also a refreshing absence of false modesty, of false self-depreciation, and of hypo-crisy whether of the Stiggins variety or the more unconscious *hypocrisie anglaise*. If Russians indulge in self-depreciation they do it with wholehearted abandonment; they seem to have little small coin of this kind. And when, as they often do, they blind themselves to distasteful facts, it is not often for puritanical reasons. The absence of hypocrisy does not mean that Russians cannot boast, cheat, wheedle, bluff, and show every kind of cunning in the market-place, or to gain an end; it merely means that they are less embarrassed at being found out. One might say that they feel they are genuine even when they are being deceitful; they are not trying to deceive you *about themselves*, and can therefore be excused.

It is the same quality that makes Russians so pleasantly free from self-importance. Their dignity, in the best of them, is natural, but except on great occasions they do not stand on their dignity. The quality of 'presence', so prized among the governing classes of many Western countries, is in Russia more typical of the actor, the singer, or the dancer, and if one tries to gauge either the rank or the impressability of other Soviet citizens by the degree of 'presence' they exhibit one will fall into sad errors. The freedom from self-importance means, too, that Russians (apart from some inflated officials) are not easy to flatter as individuals, though many of them will soak up flattery about their country.

It is this truth-to-feeling that has earned Russians the reputation, through their writers best known abroad, of being a people abandoned to melancholy. But this is true only in the sense that Russians may abandon themselves to melancholy when they feel they have good cause. At the end of last century Mackenzie Wallace judged the widespread melancholy among the peasants to be due to nothing more spiritual than the exhaustion induced by Church fasts, of which so many fall during the summer, when Russian peasants must put forth every ounce of effort. The traditional long-term optimism of the Russian peasant is much less recognized abroad than his capacity for hopelessness and resignation, yet both are to be found in Russian literature before the Revolution; if the impression of hopelessness prevails over the other, it is probably because Russian literature was so consciously concerned with exposing poverty and backwardness. *Nichevo* is understood in the West as the equivalent of 'Don't care' or 'Kismet', but it also means 'Never mind'; it is the word to shake off misfortunes and contretemps like drops of water. It is a word to express the resilience and cheerful stoicism of which Russians are capable, as it is also the word enabling them to rub along in the frank acknowledgment of their despair.

It is still true that when Russians have cause for grief or sadness they hide their feelings less than the English do. When I went to live in Kuibyshev, five hundred miles away from the front line, in the middle of the war, one of my first impressions was that people were more obviously shocked by the war than we appeared to be in Britain. There was little of the sophisticated Cockney levity on the surface of their enormous endurance and resignation; for this reason much of our war literature was embarrassingly misunderstood by those Russians who read it. As to private griefs, it is still commonly assumed that black melancholy—*ivska*—is something that can come over you, perhaps for no clear reason, and though it will scarcely serve for a medical certificate, your friends and associates will sympathize with you until it has passed off, just as when you are suffering the milder affliction which brings forth the word *skutchno*. And as to the more intrinsic melancholy of which Tchehov is the poet, it would be unnatural if a people so sensitive to personal situations had lost the power to feel sadness at the tide of life flowing inexorably by. This sadness I have certainly heard voiced in Soviet Russia by some of the middle-aged, and once by a woman as young as thirty. But the other kind of melancholy, which Tchehov treated satirically—the listlessness or fecklessness of an unoccupied class—has naturally disappeared along with the lack of occupation. It is often overlooked by Western readers how much this melancholy was a symptom of the extreme difficulty of finding an outlet for an intelligent man, of getting anything in the least degree 'political' done in Tsarist Russia. When Tchehov begged his brother to 'sweat the Asiatic out of himself', to stop sitting up at night maundering about 'having exchanged himself for cheap coin', he implied at the same time that his brother should engage in some useful activity—doctoring, perhaps, or exposing the prison conditions in Sakhalin as Tchehov did himself.

One could say that it was partly his Russian 'sincerity' which helped Dostoievsky to lay bare men's souls, but it would be wrong to conclude that Rogozhins, Grushenkas, and Mwyshkins are any commoner in Russia than in other countries. If one is tempted to take the work of any Russian writer as a whole view of Russia one must take his whole work. Even with Dostoievsky (who is not a typically Russian author, not even in his prose style) one must count alongside the great novels the idyllic sketches of young love or the humour of *Uncle's Dream* which still holds the Soviet stage; if it is Tolstoy, most capacious and most Russian of prose writers, one must count him Russian too in the didacticism which overcame his later years; if it is Tchehov one must read the dozens of light humorous sketches which first made his name, and the account of his trip to Sakhalin as well as the plays and great stories; and if it is Pushkin, most Russian of all writers and not for nothing the most popular, one must take not only the Byronic *Eugene Onegin* and *Queen of Spades* but the Mozartian passion of the love poetry, the delight in the folk strain, the anti-romanticism of such stories as 'The Snowstorm', the zestful travel sketches and the stinging obscenities.

To characterize the Russians as a people addicted to melancholy seems to me no more, and no less, true than to call them a people addicted to optimism. They are capable of abandoning themselves to either; what is striking is the sincerity and wholeheartedness of their abandonment.

When one asks Soviet refugees in England what they most miss in their exile, the answer is always on the same lines. As citizens they feel gratefully free; but in their social life they miss 'the optimism', or they miss 'the enthusiasm'; 'one cannot speak to anyone without being introduced'; 'when one has been introduced one still cannot speak *dusha-dushi* as one does in Russia— soul to soul'. And English Communists who have returned disillusioned and decommunized from living in Russia have also sometimes regretted exchanging the 'broad' Russian nature for the more reserved and channelled habits in which they had themselves been brought up.

The average Russian can be plunged for long periods into moods of either pessimism or optimism, either apathy or concentrated effort, and under the stimulus of persons around him he can also change his moods rapidly and show that they are changed, yet he cannot be called volatile or superficial. The root self-confidence and the security in his community are always underneath. The ease with which a Russian expresses his feelings (or equally his apathy and absence of feeling) has earned him the reputation with some of being 'emotional' and with others of being 'inert'. But one does not have the impression with Russians, as with some nations, of a great head of emotional steam generated internally, continually driving its victims down to the depths, irritating them into excitement, or buoying them up on clouds of ecstasy. Russians rarely appear to enjoy great exudations of feeling for the sake of feeling, and their changes in feeling seem to be intimately related to outside situations and persons. So that though it may be true, as I suggested, that it is the infant upbringing and the looseness of the Russian community which allows the individual to behave so freely, it is also to some extent true that the spontaneous and natural behaviour of individuals is what makes the loose and at the same time secure Russian community. The 'sincerity' and the community feeling seem to make an integrated system, in which each is an effect and each a cause.

There is, however, one important Russian trait which may seem to lie outside the community-individual interrelationship. This is the well-known tendency of many Russians to break out, at long intervals, into wild outbursts of joy or grief, anger, drunkenness, cruelty, or in times of war and revolution into pillage or rape. These orgiastic outbursts are brief: the yellow-moustached peasant beating his sleigh horse to death on the icy bank of the Volga—(it was his own horse and he must have known he was killing it); the normally good-natured policeman who first endured an insistent drunk, then suddenly flung him against a wall and picked him up savagely to fling him at the wall again; the usually inert neighbours who got in a goose and a store of vodka and gave a wild party for all comers; even the crass and inane violence of some of the occupation troops or of peasants during the Revolution—none of these flare-ups lasts for long. Grievances are hardly ever nursed; an orgy implies a long period of uncomplaining austerity to follow. Let champagne be poured today, instead of water, upon the stones of the bath-house to raise an intoxicating steam; tomorrow and for three months after we can manage on black bread and water!

Such outbursts seem to be accepted by Russians as part of the pattern of social behaviour, however much they may deplore some of the results. (The Church and the Mir regarded them rather as excusable safety-valves.) An outbreak is not taken to imply that a man is morally unreliable, or that there are dangerous fires smouldering beneath his usually good-natured or apathetic exterior. It is assumed that there must be an external reason for touching off the safety-valve, and this was certainly true of all the instances that I witnessed or heard of. The reason for the accumulation of passion behind the safety-valve is more difficult to explain, however. Probably these orgiastic outbreaks are different in kind rather than in degree from the more normal Russian manner of giving way to one's feelings. But as to their origin the evidence would so far seem insufficient to judge whether they are due, as Mr Geoffrey Gorer has suggested, to the rigid discipline of infant swaddling alternating with the half-hour's freedom allowed the baby at each feed, or to a complex of causes of which the swaddling is part. (Swaddling is in any case now much less usual.)

Whatever the origin of these outbursts, it is certain that their combination with the typical abandonment to spells of feeling produces one of the most significant features of Russian behaviour —that abandonment to the thing in hand which makes it difficult for so many Russians to keep regular habits unless they are obliged, which makes them careless of detailed preparation and often scornful of those addicted to it, and yet capable of bouts of long-continued activity which are beyond the endurance of the ordinary Westerner. The comparative lack of childhood discipline seems to mean that self-discipline, if applied later, is likely itself to be comparatively undisciplined.

This can be as true of the Russians who impose the discipline of the Soviet state as of the rest of their countrymen, of whom many spend a good deal of energy in trying to avoid the discipline.

In official life, for example, this means that whether one is a native or a foreigner it is a common experience, after having waited several weeks to get through to the proper authority, to be eventually summoned for a conference at perhaps an hour's notice, when one is expected to be ready with a whole dossier of plans and information with which not the slightest help had been offered earlier. The Soviet methods of concentrating on 'campaigns' and 'targets', of putting first things first and the rest nowhere, seem to derive quite as much from ancient Russian habit as from totalitarian organization.

In private life not many Russians are punctual or careful about appointments. One Soviet Russian who was punctilious in this respect was asked by her friends: 'Are you becoming an American or an Englishwoman or something, with all this fuss about appointments?' When a Russian gives you an invitation he means you to come; he is not indulging in a mere formula of courtesy, as can happen in Spain or Italy or Jugoslavia. But if you arrive an hour late he will not as a rule complain, nor will he expect you to be much disturbed if he does not himself turn up within the same period. If he forgets to come, he will be honest and say so.

Some of the most cultured Russians I knew were not embarrassed at going out with a three days' growth of beard, or at receiving callers when they were still in bed; and for my part I had not to be embarrassed if they chose to call on me for breakfast, or to telephone at 2.0 a.m. to ask the meaning of a word in an Elizabethan text. Even privileged visitors whom the authorities wish to impress are often conducted on the same happy-go-lucky principles. Select parties in the 1950's have found themselves bumping over earth roads for five hours to visit an institution in detail, listening to long speeches, and bumping back for another five hours with no food for that day between breakfast and midnight; on the following day, perhaps, banquet might follow banquet more closely than any Western digestion can endure, and then one would be wakened out of an exhausted sleep at 4.0 a.m. to take a half-day flight in a plane where no one had thought to trim the load, and the luggage stacked on the port side made the craft fly the whole distance as though about to make a banking turn.

For everyday illustration of Russian slapdashery one need go no further than the handling of money. It would seem convenient, when all currency above the value of a penny is paper, to keep the notes flat for easy handling, but this seems to be thought unnecessary fuss. Notes are crumpled anyhow in a pocket or bag, and the conductress or shopgirl pecks around in a greasy confusion to find your change.

The Russian at work, if not under discipline, can be as irregular, as intermittently enthusiastic, as when he is at leisure. He may like to start work several hours late if this is possible, but he will also stay up all night either for the satisfaction of finishing a job or to oblige someone whom he likes. A Russian carpenter working with the most limited tools, or a peasant with nothing but an axe, can quickly improvise serviceable furniture, packing-cases, doors, or cupboards. They are not merely rough, however, but rougher than one would expect—adequate but clumsy, or defective in some small irritating way. When the carpenter gets better tools he works faster but his work has similar faults, as though he could not be bothered to be more accurate. It is not the skill which is lacking but the impulse to be more skilled, more finished, than the situation is deemed to require. This was a characteristic defect in Tsarist Russia too. But when skill and care are essential one is likely to get them, just as the German traveller Kohl found over a century ago in St Petersburg where, he wrote:

The most ordinary peasants, picked up quite at random, will be charged with the transport of the costliest and most fragile articles; for example, looking-glasses, porcelain, etc., and will execute the commission with as much dexterity as if it had been their employment from childhood.

The Russian peasant, he declared, would pack and transport a quantity of glass with far fewer breakages than a German peasant could achieve. There has always been fine craftwork among Russian peasants of some districts; the minute painting on lacquer of Palekh and Mstyora is still carried on and admired today. There is nothing un-Russian about it. Neither is there anything un-Russian about the craftsmanship of such men as the toolmakers whose skill lies behind Soviet planes and fine machinery.

Yet things are still left to rust out of doors, in up-to-date air liners the lavatories can be unspeakable, the general slatternliness persists alongside the most recent devices. One begins to suspect that untidiness, inefficiency, and the so often neglected appearance of towns and people cannot be altogether due to shortages of materials or of labour nor even to laziness; they must be due at least in part to a positive quality—to the undiscriminating energy and the undiscriminating concentration with which most Russians go about things. The dislike of being finicky and the desire to get on with what seems important cause gaps, fudges, untidiness, and mistakes which exasperate a Westerner and in the end lead to trouble which even Russians are obliged to acknowledge and to clear up.

I once discussed the nature of this chaotic strain with a Moscow friend who was, it seemed to me, the wisest Russian I had ever met. Too balanced to give the usual excuses of 'reconstruction' or Bolshevik tempo, he acknowledged the strain in himself as well as in the national character, but professed himself unable to suggest its origin. 'We are an extraordinary people', he said: 'we can defeat the German armies but we cannot organize the exits from a railway station.'

After a long stay in Russia foreigners usually reach much the same impasse of judgment. And then one may come across such a passage as this:

. . . a great event, which does not *seem* great, which takes place without any 'effects', without any heroic embellishment; but it is just in that that its strength consists. This simplicity, of which, perhaps, no other nation in the world has the conception, is the very peculiarity of the Russian nation. Everything is simple, everything appears to be even less significant than it is. Innocence—that is also a peculiarity of the Russian soul. A great exploit is accomplished 'innocently'. O, who will understand the greatness of this simplicity, before which all the world's great exploits will fade?

This was written in the eighteen-forties by the Slavophil

Konstantin Aksakov, who dealt in such un-Marxist abstractions as 'inner truth' and 'conscience', great Russian virtues which he opposed to the concepts of 'external law' and 'coercion' which for him were typical of Western ideas. And the passage was reprinted for approval and for inspiration in the most popular of Soviet magazines, *Ogonyok*, while the war was still in progress.

Can it be that the Bolsheviks not only admit but admire this 'innocent' simplicity? After all, most Bolsheviks are Russians. Aksakov has expressed perfectly the quality which has so often captivated foreigners—the vast generosity and goodness with vague edges, the simplicity of Levin in *Anna Karenina* or Prince Mwyshkin, the beautiful directness of Russian folk tunes, the humanity of films like *The Road to Life* or *My Universities*. . . .

It is a quality which can appeal like a revelation to people brought up in more puritanical or more self-conscious societies. It is a quality which insulates admirably against some of the dehumanizing effects of industrial life. But in its very humanity it insulates also against much of the objectivity which modern life demands. It can become a maddening quality to Westerners who have to work with Russians for a long time. When one has become thoroughly used to their un-English warmth, their uncritical satisfaction with the world of personal relationships, and the way they float as nonchalant individuals having some invisible umbilical connection with each other—when one has become thoroughly used to all this one feels how defective, in so many of them, is the interest in or respect for objects, for objects in all their concreteness and inexorability.

Russian personalities, for example, rarely enshrine themselves in their household gods. When you see a Russian family acquiring a wardrobe and taking it home by hired lorry it is an ecstatic event that a family of that kind, for the first time in history, should possess a wardrobe. But call two years later and you may well find the wardrobe scratched and uncared for. Its owners will value it for its serviceability, or possessively perhaps as the idea of a wardrobe, but they do not feel that they owe it to themselves, or to the neighbours, or to the wardrobe, to treasure it with more care. The new buildings of Moscow University have magnificent halls and equipment, but the less grandiose staircases, the ones which are in use every day, show much more deterioration than one should expect after only six years' use. Someone did not take trouble enough over them. Thousands of Soviet vacuum cleaners are now being produced; they work well enough until a small part breaks. It is a part said to cost only 75 kopecks, but you cannot buy another; no one has organized spares, and your machine is useless.

Is it where objects and facts are concerned that Russians are not always as 'sincere' with themselves as they might be? In the West we tend to self-deception and hypocrisy about our own natures in respect of our relations with others, while we seem to be franker judges of our own natures, on the whole, in respect of our relations with the world of objects.

With Russians the characteristics are perhaps reversed. Because of their upbringing they are more inclined to a true view of themselves in their human relations than we are; their Self is not to be thrown in the face of others as in many Western countries; it is when they come to the world of objects that that Self is allowed such freedom for its natural vigour that the true nature of the object itself may not always be apprehended. The Self may demand to be admired for its *élan* and its intention, while the concrete result, perhaps imperfect, may take a secondary place.

Russians have wonderful 'attack'. One has only to see a crowd of peasants charging purposefully out of a Moscow terminus to realize that. It is the discipline of the attack which Russians find difficult. Dame Ninette de Valois writes in her autobiography that when she was training with the Diaghileff Ballet she found her 'projection and general attack faint in comparison with the Russians' and her 'personality reserved', but—

Russians can be astonishingly inaccurate in their repetition of any set movement, and thus the sustaining of Russian vitality is free from the tiring restraint of discipline and accuracy; they are consistently concerned with the uninhibited projection of themselves . . . sometimes the projection of their energy is not distributed equally between the physical and the mental. . . .

Before the Revolution Russians were best known in the West through the intelligentsia and their propensity for discussion, for peeling away layer after layer of a situation in order to discuss its essence, instead of launching into action which might have only a pragmatic sanction. But the contrary process—the rushing into action without adequate discussion or consideration—is equally Russian. During the disturbances of 1906 the peasants of the Kherson district burnt down the house of a generous and popular landlord. When he remonstrated with them they said: '*Barin*, we decided to set fire to your house just because you are the best landowner in these parts, and so we should show that we are acting on principle and not in a spirit of vengeance.' (Rothay Reynolds—*My Russian Year*, 1913.) It is easy to think of parallel examples in some of the precipitate or megalomaniac actions of the early Five-Year Plans—the beginning of great buildings on marshy ground which would make their completion impossible, or the first campaign for collectivization in the villages, when the directives were blunt enough and many of the young Russians who carried them out were blunter still. In the campaign for Lysenko's theories (which are still not abandoned) there would seem to be both a premature resort to action and a superfluous intellectual element in the desire to rationalize simple acts of agricultural policy in doctrinal form.

It is a triumph of Russian energy and attack that the Soviet Government has succeeded in imposing the disciplines of technology upon so many millions, and in inspiring the best of these to develop techniques further. When one works with ordinary Russians one finds on the one hand a narrow and finicky adherence to technique or rule, and on the other hand a tendency to short cuts and improvisation with little regard for matters of detail, finish, or maintenance. Both characteristics are going to persist for a very long time before, if ever, an adjusted, practical, middle path becomes normal. Both of them involve a certain failure to come to grips with the objective world, and though they have been organized to produce some of the greatest Soviet triumphs, they have also contributed to some of the most inhuman aspects of the régime.

5

Russian Society—The Mass

Every Russian when he is among Englishmen at once feels at home, though he may not be like them in character, beliefs, or education. And you will be told of the corresponding feeling by every Englishman who has lived in Russia, but not by the Frenchman, the German, or the Italian.

WHEN Nicholas Homyakov, President of the Third Duma, expressed this rather surprising opinion, the last of the Tsars was still on his throne, and the few Englishmen who made a long stay in Russia were usually merchants or gentlemen with a taste for country sports. After the Revolution these were succeeded by technicians, journalists, and visitors whose interests were almost inevitably political. It was hardly possible to go to look at Russia any more: one went to look at Communism.

Yet, whatever else the Revolution has changed it has made very little difference to the impression made by Russians, as people, upon Englishmen who live some time in their country and learn their language. The Englishman may leave Russia under deep political disillusionment, he may feel himself culturally nearer to the French, the Swedes, or the Italians, but underneath the dingy Russian exterior he still discovers, as his predecessors did, that in personal relationships and general attitude to life the English have more in common with the Russians than with many nations nearer home.

The Russian ways of avoiding social friction, the Russian sense of humour, the Russian attitude to women, and that recent development, Russian sportsmanship—they all seem nearer to the English than the Latin world. The convention of good manners in Russia, as in Britain, is that there are few conventions: good intent is what counts, and one can penetrate to a Russian's intention directly, instead of having to peer at them through a cage of strange behaviour. The social atmosphere in Russia is streaked with childish optimism or exasperating fatalism from time to time, but it is free from the cynicism about human nature which can so offend the English in Mediterranean or Levantine company. In the Russians the Englishman recognizes something resembling his own idealism, blended with a great capacity for being practical. And though Russians and English will disagree shockingly about the occasions when it is appropriate to be idealistic and the occasions when it is appropriate to be practical, they agree in not being hampered by Latin assumptions about the all-importance of form, nor by German preoccupations with finish and discipline for their own sakes.

It would be natural for an English visitor to assume that a people with whom he has so much in common should develop the same sort of social 'climate' as he is used to at home. But here the common ground between English and Russian comes to an end. One discovers by degrees that the resemblance between so many Russian and English characteristics is not derived from resemblance between the two societies; the resemblance is largely a coincidence, and the history of the two societies has been too dissimilar for it to be otherwise. In fact it is rather remarkable that there should be so much in common between the English on the one hand, with their tradition of child discipline, their six or seven hundred years of free private enterprise, and their 150 years of town-bred sophistication, and on the other hand the Russians, whose children are not disciplined and who are most of them but one generation away from a stage of society which was dying out in England six centuries ago. The traits which we have in common could be of importance if Russians and English could meet more freely; yet even if that were possible the differences between our societies, quite apart from our political differences, would not cease to be significant. And the roots of the social differences go back very far—as far, indeed, as there is any record of the Russian people.

Ancient Russian society must have presented a satisfactory world picture to frame the hard and monotonous lives of the peasants. They lived in the tribe 'as in a great family', (even into the nineteenth century in some places) under the authority of a patriarchal head. Kinship was the root of their social organization, and the *rod* or clan seems to have been more powerful than the *semya* or family in the modern sense. They had specific names for persons of the most distant relationship, as many Africans and Asians have today. Even in the twentieth century peasants were still using some of these kinship names which had become forgotten among educated Russians. Names of kinship were also used as signs of brotherhood or of respect when addressing those who were not kindred, and to this day, whether it is a shy village child making friends or a town urchin flinging dirty words at a stranger, Russian children call elders 'uncle' or 'aunt'. Adults may still address any stranger of roughly their own age and position as 'brother', while the old are addressed in a friendly manner as *batushka* or *matushka*—terms which are too literally rendered, in most translations from Russian novels, as 'little father' and 'little mother'; they are just rather more elegant but classless equivalents of the working-class English 'dad' and 'ma'.

The old Russian's ancestors were part of the great family too: their souls inhabited trees—not the forbidding firs but the beautiful, longer-lived birch trees which have such symbolic importance in Russian folk rhyme and song. Their spirits, we are told by the Soviet Academician Y. M. Sokolov, were still being invoked in protection of the house or speeding of the harvest, just before the Revolution of 1917. Ancestor and parent relationships determined so much of a man's own brief span that

the consciousness of personality, of its own ways, vocations, and rights developed tardily and slowly on the Russian soil both in pagan and in Christian times. This is the deepest religious root of Russian collectivism. (George Fedotov, in *The Russian Religious Mind*, Harvard, 1946.)

In the ancient tribe the Russian was surrounded by more than human uncles. Fields, forest, rivers, and *izbas* all had patronal deities or semi-deities in the form of an 'Old Man', while streams were often haunted by the *Rusalki*, or spirits of drowned maidens. The Old Man of the House, the *domovoi*, might occasionally be glimpsed as a warm woolly creature, but he was cross if you tried to catch a sight of him. He had to be propitiated at intervals, and when you moved house it was calamitous not to take him with you by removing some of the embers from the old house to the new. In the nineteen-twenties the American journalist Rhys Williams found the *domovoi* still ruling the lives of many older peasants; when a new cow was bought it had to be of the right colour or 'the house-master wouldn't like it'. As for *Dyed Moroz* or Jack Frost ('Old Man Frost'), he survives into almost official status as the Soviet equivalent of Santa Claus; every year in snowy costume he distributes the New Year presents from thousands of New Year trees in schools and clubs.

Into these ancient beliefs the institutions of the Church seem to have been grafted, from the eleventh century onwards, with the usual undercover rivalry between old gods and new. (There were still prosecutions for paganism in the twentieth century.) The peasants, to judge by all accounts, regarded the priest or 'pope' as in daily life somewhat less than a whole man, but as the necessary personage for births, weddings, funerals, and a few other occasions. Ceremonial observance was more important than doctrine, and the wrestlings of individual conscience mattered less than the sharing in the community life of the church services, where there was something of the same feeling of brotherhood as in the gatherings of the Mir which settled so many secular problems for you, no one knew quite how. In the Russian Church children participate in all sacraments from the age of six or so. From that age they take part in confession, the significance of which seems to be the restoring of the penitent to the community rather than the cleansing of an individual erring soul. Repentance restores you to the fold, but if you do not sin you cannot repent. You have little privacy in confession and you confess to sins, named by the priest, of which you are not consciously guilty, for in doing so you confess your part in the common nature of unregenerate mankind.

The blend of Christian and pre-Christian beliefs and customs was buttressed with enough fatalism to stand the shocks of recurrent famine, the imposition of complete serfdom, the impact of its abolition in 1861, the tyranny of bad landlords, and the invasions of superior authority which haled off young men to military service for as long as twenty-five years. The village preserved the memories of those who had seen all this come and go, who had seen Tatars retreat and Napoleon's armies defeated by patient endurance and native cunning, and the total result bred a stoical optimism at least as powerful as the fatalism which might seem to us a more natural response. There is more optimism than gloom in the Russian folk-stories, more triumph than terror, and among the peasant characters of classical Russian literature figures of noble example, such as Leskov's Enchanted Pilgrim, are commoner than creatures of hopelessness and passivity.

From the late eighteenth century onwards there was some dilution of the peasant and handicraft character of Russian society. A small number of peasants were diverted to become town 'proletarians'—just enough of them to make a class-conscious soil for revolutionary groups in the 1900's. An increasing number of peasants made themselves traders or merchants, and after the Emancipation of 1861 this new bourgeois class began to be increased by the addition of some independent peasant farmers— the 'strong and sober' whom the Tsarist land reforms were meant to encourage. Then there was a small but growing intelligentsia, recruited from the smaller gentry, the trading class, and the bureaucracy. Most of them looked avidly to the West, and they had many un-Russian ways of behaviour; their families seem to have been smaller than the average and the upbringing of them less traditional. Over all flourished as for centuries past the sprawling life of the nobles, which with its untidy families and its country nannies came perhaps nearer to the peasants than the life of either the trading class or the intelligentsia. But the new classes and their new ideas had not spread far under the Tsarist despotism when war and revolution descended on a nation which was still four-fifths peasant.

It seems to be regularly forgotten, in a world so long overhung by fear of Bolshevism, that the Russian Revolution of March 1917 *was not made by the Bolsheviks.* Three years of exhausting and incompetently-conducted war had brought millions of peasant soldiers and their officers tramping home to fight no more, and to share in the orgy of liberation which the March Revolution signified for every class in Russia except the Royal Family. It was a Revolution which 'simply happened' because no one would support the autocracy any more. All over Russia the peasants seized the land and burnt the great houses; they had been burning down an average of fifty a year all over Russia for more than a century, but this time there was no retribution. A liberal (but unelected) government under Kerensky introduced universal suffrage and made speeches, but it dithered about the two questions that mattered most—peace and the land. And then in October the smallest of the political parties, the Bolshevik Party, was able to seize power because of its compact and determined leadership and because it was the only group which appeared to know its own mind. (The 'October' Revolution is the one which has been celebrated every year since, on 7th November.) Other political parties were almost immediately banned, and nationalization and expropriation began. But before they could much affect the masses of the people the Revolution was brought home to all in the worse agonies of the Civil War, the War of Intervention, and the regional famines which accompanied or followed them.

A breathing-space—the period of the New Economic Policy—gave small trade and manufacture an opportunity to make life barely tolerable again, while major measures of socialization and the strengthening of the Party hold continued. And then, in the First Five-Year Plan of 1928-32, industrialization on a socialized basis, and the political dictatorship to guarantee it, were forced into the pattern of Russian life, never to leave it. Yet what happened was not only the expropriation of private trade and industry, the brutal collectivization of the farms, and the 'liquidation of the kulaks as a class'. What happened was also part of the worldwide transformation from immemorial agricultural society to a new and uncharted industrial society in which no one can say how many of the old ways will hold. (In Russia the transformation had already acquired much impetus under capitalist conditions during the years 1905 to 1911.)

The First Five-Year Plan was dramatized and publicized so as to win admiration far outside the Soviet Union. Some of it was carried out by forced labour, and some by enthusiastic and untrained young people who got into unheated freight trains and went off to build steelworks in uninhabited wastes, or railways across icy deserts. Students and others in towns gave their unskilled labour free in evenings and on 'rest days'. Young workers did double shifts for single pay in order to advance the Plan. They were still doing so in 1934 when I had friends among the builders of the Moscow Metro. But these were the more sophisticated ones. Millions of peasants took to industrialism in a naïve enthusiasm, as English country people did in the early 1800's, glad to get a steady job under a roof in winter, or fascinated by town life and the new machines. Peasants streamed into the towns, in summer sleeping in the streets, in stations, in areas and backyards. Many floated from one job to another, untrained for any. There was one year when the Soviet coalmines had a labour turnover of over 100 per cent. As late as 1943 I talked to a high railway official who sighed with envy when he heard that English railway workers usually stick to their jobs for life.

There was nothing peculiarly Russian in these irresponsible attitudes. An Englishman writing in the early nineteenth century of the factories in his own country said: 'The real difficulty lay in training human beings to renounce their desultory habits of work.' But in Britain we have forgotten the stages by which these habits were overcome.

Quite apart from the rigours of political dictatorship it was naturally by the most painful trial and error that the need for habits of work discipline was generally realized, or that simple people progressed beyond knocking in screws with a hammer 'in order to fulfil the Plan more quickly'. Ten years after the beginning of the Five-Year Plans, labour laws were introduced to tie men and women to a particular job and to punish unpunctuality, unauthorized absences, and other 'offences against labour discipline'. (These measures were relaxed only in 1956, and mobility is reported great since then.) But against these compulsive methods, and others such as the organization of railway workers into quasi-military units, one should count the training of a generation of technicians. It was of minor significance, in the emergency, that many of the training courses appeared to foreign technicians to be too specialized and *ad hoc*; it was this training, given to workers of every age and either sex, which saved Soviet industrialization.

Failures and breakdowns naturally continued—in manufacture, in transport, in power supply, in retail distribution, in agriculture. The ruling oligarchy saw counter-revolution behind every bush, they feared for their personal positions and often mistrusted their own colleagues, and they were as prone as the masses under them to the national vice of confusing intention and performance. 'Sabotage' and 'wrecking' were perhaps to be expected from the dispossessed, the collectivized, or the merely disgruntled, but they became accusations to fit any case of failure or breakdown or the showing of initiative which might be a threat to some aspect of the all-pervading 'line'. There were executions and purges before Stalin seized power; they came and went in waves, but it was not till December 1934 that Stalin decided to secure his position for good by the terror of the 'mass purges'. By these, it is now clear, he intended to pay off private scores, to remove possible rivals, and to frighten the nation into complete submission. No one was now safe from denunciation for acts of momentary carelessness, for lack of enthusiasm, for enthusiasm at the wrong moment, for having the wrong friends or the wrong parents, or for merely being in such a position that he was bound to be denounced. An official report cites as a typical instance how

Gladkikh, former secretary of the district committee of the Party in

Rodvino, Archangel Region, instructed every Communist to discover an enemy of the people.

Those in authority showered denunciations right and left to show their zeal but this did not protect many of them—even the heads of the whole security organization—from denunciation and execution themselves. Some tried desperately to insure themselves with the aid of a medical certificate:

Owing to the state of his health and mind Comrade X is not fit to be used as a tool by any class enemy.

> District Psychiatrist,
> October District,
> City of Kiev.

At last the terror died down, and the glum-faced Beria became head of security until his own execution in 1954. After the mass purges there were but three years of material, and to a certain extent political, relaxation before the second war with Germany, the most bloody and exhausting in all the Russian history of invasions. Twenty million dead and twenty-five million homeless are now the official figures, only released fourteen years after the war ended. In addition unofficial figures estimate that over the whole Stalin period something like one family in two had one of its members spending years in a prison camp.

One might expect Russians to be reduced to a nation of cowed, disintegrated units after nearly forty years of such suffering. On the surface there is nowadays a certain amount of nonchalance, and a tendency to mind one's own business. And yet, apart from a fringe of hooligans and rootless persons living on their wits, beneath these impressions the Russians still convey an overwhelming sense of a people of great cohesion who take 'family' relationship for granted in their ordinary living. Old beliefs may have disappeared but social relationships have persisted.

In their new industrial life the Russians are not merely overcrowded in the flat, share of a flat, or share of a room which they may occupy in a large block; they may spend almost the whole of their time in overclose proximity to the same persons, whether at work, at play, or at home. The apartment block is very often attached to the place of work, the necessary shops are incorporated in its base, and within the same set of buildings is likely to be the club, exclusive to that enterprise, which provides the most convenient entertainment—sometimes better entertainment than is to be had by the general public.

The millions of young technicians in training, and many of the young unmarried workers, must live in even closer association, in an *obshchezhitie* or communal dormitory, where the beds may be packed so tightly together that there is hardly room to pass between. They keep their few belongings in cupboards and lead a sober, decorous life in the dormitory, where there may be shift workers asleep somewhere right through the twenty-four hours. Yet foreign workers who have lived in these places have told me of their surprise at the small amount of friction, and the uncomplaining acceptance of such a close-packed way of living.

It is true that these conditions are mostly the result of sheer physical necessity; if one insisted on waiting for a fullsize flat of one's own one would never get out of the *obshchezhitie*, and the alternative to a holiday in a crowded 'rest camp' or 'sanatorium' might well be no holiday at all. But the impressive fact is that, apart from a more sensitive minority, Russians do not seem to feel that enforced close company is the same threat to individual identity that we ourselves would feel; the lack of physical elbow-room does not seem to mean a lack of elbow-room for the spirit.

The simple mass ways of living make a striking impression on a Westerner, and whether he approves of them or not he is almost bound at first to assume that the Soviet Government is responsible for the communal feeling which pervades them all. If he is sympathetic to the régime he imagines he has discovered the kind of unselfregarding behaviour which ought to result from socialism; if he is unsympathetic then he has discovered the 'regimentation' which he expected. But both these views accept the official story too readily. The Soviet explanation is that the communal spirit has been released by getting rid of the individualistic, distintegrating influence of the capitalist stage of Russian history. But the capitalist influence was brief and limited in Russia. When the visitor has seen some village life for himself, and read some Russian history, when he has made some contacts in the middle of Russian crowds and has discussed his impressions with a few of the more analytic Russians, and when he has seen how Russian children are brought up, he can have no doubt that the old semi-conscious village feeling has transplanted itself, if somewhat weakened by the removal, into industrial surroundings.

When Russian exiles nowadays revisit their country after forty or fifty years they usually admire the great improvement in the standard of living, they find themselves disoriented in some respects, but they recognize the old spirit among the Russian people with delight. 'The people in Soviet cities', said one old exile, are 'tot zhe samy chutky, mily, otzychivy, gostepriimny narod . . .'—'the same considerate, responsive, nice, hospitable people that they always were.'

The Russian 'family' tradition is not difficult for a foreigner to feel, but elusive to define. It does not mean that Russians are not moved by self-interest or do not show initiative; Russian peasants have long been famous for both, and the modern Russian is a great improviser. Neither does it mean that Russians are vastly concerned for the common good, except in occasional waves like other peoples. Why should such a vigorous nation never have developed to any great extent the individual enterprise, the individual sense of responsibility and the individual self-sufficiency, let alone the self-esteem and the aggressive self-assertion which to many Western peoples seem second nature?

The fact is that while Russian history has been strong in forces tending to preserve the traditional collective life, it has always been weak in forces which could develop the status and rights of the individual. And these forces have not merely been weak because collective forces were strong; they have simply been lacking or almost lacking. So that if we come from the West we cannot too often remind ourselves how slight has been the impression made in Russia by the ideas and institutions which helped to build what we now consider as the 'Western' outlook—how little Russia has experienced of the attitudes of the Western Churches, the Roman idea of the rule of law, the independent peasant farming of the West, and the colossal growth of trade and commerce over the last three or four hundred years.

The Western Churches' view of the human person is so deeply ingrained in the consciousness of all of us in the West, whether we call ourselves believers or not, that it comes sometimes as a shock to realize that there can be another attitude calling itself Christian.

In the first centuries of the Christian faith it was Eastern theologians, nurtured in the traditions of Greek philosophy, who laid the foundations of all Christian theology, while the later, Roman, contribution came from men bred more in the atmosphere of Roman law. From the fifth century onwards it was the Western Church which gradually laid more stress on the human nature in Christ, while the East laid more on the divine nature and on the transcendental aspect of the Almighty. The West came to cultivate the values of the individual human being, who should strive to follow in the footsteps of Jesus. The East believed that the Divine Nature was accessible, by the greatest efforts, to ascetics, who were presumed to lead the highest form of Christian life, while to the ordinary person it might be accessible through the sacraments. The Orthodox service is long, it appeals to all the senses, and at the most exalted moments of the ceremonies it is held that worshippers may, through all their senses, be in touch with Deity itself. The Russian had not to seek the 'imitation of Christ'; that was a Western idea. The Spirit descended upon him when, *in common with his fellows*, he was taking part in the divine ceremony. If he wished to cultivate personal holiness, it was mainly with the idea of making himself a more fitting vessel for revelation when it should come. What matters is to keep the pure and living spirit of the early days of Christianity, just as the five domes have always been obligatory for every Russian church building, on the model of the earliest church in Jerusalem. Orthodoxy, as Berdyaev has pointed out, 'educates the heart rather than the will'.

In the West men of intellect hammered at the laws of thought in order to refute the heretic and to demonstrate that the intellect also, as well as conscience and heart and spirit, finds its answer within the Christian religion. But it would have seemed a contamination of the true faith to attempt such work in countries of the Orthodox Church. Eventually the human intellect and spirit became so cultivated in the West that they began to burst the bonds of any Mother Church. The Reformation and later Nonconformist movements asserted not merely the duty of individual Christians to follow in the way of Christ, but also their right to judge for themselves the nature and meaning of that Way. Diverging further from the traditionalism of the East, they declared more and more boldly that God is not to be captured in any ritual, place, or form, and that the search for Him must be unending. From this it was no great step to freethinking or to modern humanism, and yet the roots go back to the fifth century.

In Russia there were Nonconformist sects too, but most of them were fundamentalist or reactionary. If the most precious experience for an Orthodox Christian depends upon the sacraments, then the ancient forms involved in their celebration must be preserved in every detail. So when in 1654 the Russian Patriarch Nikon introduced the mildest possible reforms in the church services—corrections, in part, of ancient unscholarly errors—there was an uproar, and a large number of the faithful seceded, to become known as the Old Believers. Their nonconformity and the persecutions which they suffered gave them much the same austere virtues as the Western Nonconformists. They still have a few churches in Soviet Russia, being noted among other things for their ban on tobacco. But their stiffneckedness and austerity have been on the whole too conservative and clannish to contribute much to the growth of individual freedom in Russia.

Although today the Church has little influence in Russian society, yet the kind of consciousness bred by the Russian Church has not lost its part in the consciousness of both the rulers of Russia and the ruled. Just as the spirit of Western Christianity still helps to breed independence in a Western freethinker, the spirit of Orthodox Christianity, along with the spirit of the Mir and even of the *rod*, still help to breed in Russians their conviction that in the common sharing of an experience—divine in church worship, man-made in Communist achievement—they preserve a truer humanity than a Westerner can partake of in his over-cultivation of the individual.

In Western Europe the Christian sense of individuality began to be reinforced, in the later Middle Ages, by the establishment of courts of law where the ordinary citizen, or at any rate most ordinary citizens, could feel some protection against despotic power, whether of the landowner, the rich, or the strong.

It is sufficient to say that Russia was entirely without institutions of this kind until the second half of the nineteenth century. Laws were made and enforced by the same power. The judicial and the administrative arms were one and the same thing until the decrees of 1862 and 1865, which set up courts on the Western model, trial by jury, and judges who were in theory irremovable. But these innovations proved too much for the autocracy to assimilate. A large number of offences, including press and 'political' offences, were presently declared to be outside the competence of a jury, and the judges found themselves to be by no means irremovable in fact. (G. Alexinsky—*Modern Russia*, 1913.) The judicial system did not depend upon the police so much as compete with it; in 1907 Sir Bernard Pares reported that 'about as many administrative arrests are still said to take place as those which take place under law'. The ordinary Russian thus had little reason to expect the judiciary to maintain his rights as an individual, and the peasant felt safer with such old customs as he had. The Mir had added to its status, though unwillingly, by becoming the State's agent in collecting taxes, and at least the Mir was familiar. At the end of the nineteenth century it still had the power of exiling its recalcitrant members to Siberia. That kind of justice seemed easier to understand than the paraphernalia of the new courts. So 'administrative arrests' continued as part of the heritage of a Russian, and the Soviet dual system of arbitrary 'political' arrests and of procedure through the courts is not new.

Not only the Western spirit of law but the whole Western spirit of enquiry was felt but feebly in Russia until the nineteenth century. There was no rising middle class to demand the new values of a Reformation as in Western Europe, and there was no impulse towards a Renaissance either. The people had their Bible and liturgy in their own language (or rather the ancient form called Church Slavonic), and the very accessibility of these essential texts was something of a barrier to further learning.

The whole development of the modern spirit—of the individual asking questions about the universe—affected Russia almost entirely as a foreign growth. She had her robust pioneers—adventurers who reached the Pacific Ocean before the end of the seventeenth century, a few original minds like Lomonosov, and others now assiduously publicized by Soviet historians. But the very publicity which has now to be given to these unrecognized pioneers provides further proof how, between the autocracy on the one hand and the feebleness of humanistic tradition on the other, they had little suitable climate to work in until the nineteenth century. In that century Russian vigour and originality, reinforced by Western ideas, were such that they often called down more autocratic repression than before. (Under Nicholas I a story was told of a mathematics textbook which was banned by the censorship because it contained such expressions as 'the series 2, 4, 8, 16, . . .' Rows of dots were prohibited because they must be libellous; anyone, it was alleged, could guess the names which they were supposed to indicate.)

Even when freer ideas penetrated Russian life they had little opportunity to reach far beyond the intelligentsia, who suffered from a surfeit, since they were prevented from realizing all but a minute number of ideas in practice. An important faction among the intelligentsia became nervous of the new importations, and without denying the need for change they tried to develop old Russian concepts and institutions into something nationally significant for their own time. These Slavophils idealized the Russian peasant, the Mir, and the far-off Kievan heroic period; though often vague and fantastic, they did useful work in educating the peasantry, and they were something of a stabilizing element in the general welter. But once again it was the old communal spirit asserting itself even among those who seemed most suitable to be inspired by the West. In the view of most Russian reformers, whatever their theories, the overwhelming need was first to relieve the backwardness and suffering of the masses. It seemed idle to spend much time agitating for liberal institutions, since only in the very long run could these help Russians as individuals to help themselves.

It is thus no invention of Soviet times for Russians to be suspicious of Western influences, though it is only since Russia became Marxist that all Western 'errors' have been attributed to our bourgeois or capitalist condition. But even if the whole Marxist analysis of our bourgeois period were correct, it would still be clear that the history of Western individualism goes back far beyond the first stirrings of anything that can be called capitalism —farther, possibly, than the fifth-century beginnings of the divergence between Eastern and Western Churches.

Yet to compare Western individualism with Russian collectivism is not to compare completely incompatible ways of looking at society. For what are considered in England, for example, as 'individual' values are in fact passionately held as communal values. To be English requires one to be a good deal *separate*, and particularly to live in separateness from others, but the fact that we observe separateness is part of our conformity, part of what identifies us as members of the English community. Being separate does not require that we should all be different from one another, and though we prize in principle the liberty to be different, we do, like other peoples, look askance at those who diverge too much from our ideas of the normal.

In Russia the essential, unspoken requirement of society in general is that people should not feel, or behave, as though they were as separate from each other as in England. They may be different from each other, but they should not be separate from each other; they should not be separate in spirit. Mackenzie Wallace tells of a sugar factory in 1903 where the government inspector was shocked at the barracklike living accommodation and insisted that partitions should be erected to give each man some privacy. But this was resented. 'Are we cattle?' asked the workers, 'that we should be thus cooped in stalls?' Today, with a higher standard of living, the vaunted single rooms in Moscow University are reported to be unpopular with students; they would prefer more communal life. And unseparateness, to the horror of the foreigner, still holds for most public lavatories, where except for the division of the sexes customers squat over holes in the floor in full view of one another.

Yet the general lack of 'partitions' has the surprising result that private life among Russians can be intensely private. There is much less physical privacy to be had than in Britain, but while in Britain one is private, so to speak, because of the partitions, in Russia one could almost be said to be private because of their absence. Erect the partitions—especially the intangible ones—between man and man, and the Russian might feel that he could not trust his neighbour. But with slight partitions or none the Russian feels that he is in the company of the same sort of person as himself, the sort of person who can be left alone. So in the congestion of flat life, ingenious devices and great forbearance are shown so as to secure a little privacy. Whether in friendly or unfriendly intercourse, neighbours or acquaintances do not invade one another's lives with the clumsy, demanding entirety of some nations; the very closeness of the community life, and the common subjection to Government pressure and interference, seem to bring out relationships of greater delicacy. For in spite of all the association at close quarters, a Russian can be left alone when he wishes to be. If he is a good Russian his neighbours know that he is not being fundamentally separate but is still 'one of us', just as the Englishman in his castle-home knows that his neighbours will in emergency cease to be separate and will come out of their castle-homes to fight as a community.

The gulf between the English attitude and the Russian attitude is perhaps after all a gulf of degree rather than of difference. But it is a profound gulf, and to my mind it would be a very long time before it could disappear. What separates us socially is, roughly speaking, the greater collectivism of the Russians. What separates us politically is collectivism, dictatorship, and the Marxist attitude to human nature. The political and the social overlap but they are not the same, and it is fundamental to understanding the Russian people to realize that they are not the same. For to the Englishman collectivism implies conformity, docility, similarity, and unseparateness. But though the Russians incline to be unseparate, and in their relationship to their own group conformist, they are little inclined to be either docile or conformist in their attitudes towards authority.

Government, in Russia, is not traditionally expected to derive its sanction from the governed, from which it follows that government, though unloved, is respected according to its efficiency and even sometimes according to its ruthlessness. But that does not imply that one co-operates with it. Russian history is full of revolts against landowners and officials, and the popular attitude was described in 1903 by the American visitor W. Greener, who found civilians siding with each other against all officials, and the least disturbance likely to become a riot: 'There seems to be', he wrote, 'not an organized but a natural opposition to the representatives of government.' One of the most remarkable facts about the Russian people is that though serfdom made them cunning, secretive, and suspicious of innovation and enterprise, it did not cow them nor even give them a chip on the shoulder. And today only a slight experience of Russian life will disabuse a foreigner of the idea that Russians have any natural tendency to do as they are ordered—still less that they feel the need to which some Germans will confess, of actually preferring to receive orders.

Soviet power is a great deal more efficient than Tsarist power ever was, and yet the average Russian reaction to the orders of officials other than the political police is still to cajole or to argue. And this includes the ordinary policeman—the 'militiaman' in Soviet terminology. There are few more instructive sights than the little crowd which can gather in protest round a militiaman dragging away a drunk who cannot keep his feet; the comrade militiaman (who can hardly keep his) is being far too rough with the citizen drunk! When one has been accepted by one's neighbours in a Soviet flat, or when one has been temporarily included in a crowd of Russian peasants, one feels admitted into a tacit conspiracy against all external authority—the old, silent, spontaneous conspiracy of peasant cunning against landlords and masters and representatives of the law. This is a conspiracy which seems to extend frequently to the protection of some kinds of criminal; in wartime it often extended to escaped German prisoners, many of whom found kindness and help at the hands of Russian peasants.

External authority to the Russians, it would seem, has always been an evil to be tolerated only because of overriding necessity, and to be concentrated so far as possible in a figure who was by definition above the whole mass of his people, not chosen by them and not accountable to them. 'It is easier to suffer injury from the Tsar than from one's brother, for he is the ruler of us both.' In early Kievan days there were only clan princes who often fought among themselves, but it was held an impious crime to kill a ruler. Then came the despotism of the Mongol khans who held down Russia for over two hundred years, yet even to this power the Church preached submission, alleging that the Mongols had been sent to punish the sins of the Russian people. The first Tsar won his power by collecting tribute on behalf of the Mongols and quietly becoming strong enough to defy them; he was not responsible to the Russians, but rather a divinely-appointed agent, and he and his successors inherited something of the distant untouchability and omnipotence of the Mongol power. The Russian nobility were divided among themselves and more concerned with the confirmation of their own privileges than with taking a hand in government. They did not develop, as they might have done during the mid-seventeenth century 'Time of the Troubles', the doctrine that the sovereign derived his power in part from them.

The idea of an authority which took any of its sanction from the people was completely outside Russian conceptions until the nineteenth century, when a minority became affected by Western ideas of representative government. But the Tsar's agents were quite a different matter from the Tsar himself. If the Tsar knew how they behaved, the peasants used to say, he would see them punished, but he could not know everything or be everywhere at once. The most useful weapon in the hands of officials was often simply the capacity to persuade the peasants that what was commanded was indeed the personal fiat and desire of the Tsar. And today, though Russians may respect the Soviet power because of its comparative effectiveness, to accept all its agents is still another thing.

For to accept these intermediaries as rulers would be to violate the ancient Russian egalitarianism. 'Unseparateness' connotes also equality of status to Russians. Except for the sacrosanct leader— or perhaps the Party—on whom one can load everything, it is mortally offensive, unbearable, for one man to set himself up as better than another or as a power over him; he may shout or give orders in the name of authority, but to arrogate power breaks down the whole community spirit, and some of the long wheedling arguments one can hear between Soviet citizens and officials are intended to demonstrate to the officials that they too are 'one of us'. The foreigners Beck and Godin, reporting on their experience among Russian political prisoners, found that the greatest insult which could be offered to a prison officer was to accuse him of *izdevatelstvo*. In spite of all the severity of prison life, officers would defend themselves indignantly against this charge—the allegation that in enforcing orders they had shown a lack of respect for some prisoner as a human being.

The lack of feeling about status has always been one of the most important lubricants in Russian life. Even children are made to feel less inferior than in many countries. In peasant Russia the Mir system involved hardly any ideas of status, and outside it there was little class structure to develop such ideas. The relationship between nobles, gentry, peasants, and others seems to have been much more of a caste system than a class system; there was no general ladder of ascent, and so jealousies about ascending it could not arise. The German J. G. Kohl wrote after visiting Russia in 1837:

There are people who believe that the lower classes in Russia are a separate and oppressed caste, without a will of their own, and without influence over their superiors; and that the civilized class floats over the mass like oil over water, neither mingling nor sympathizing with the other. Now this is the very reverse of the truth. There is perhaps no country in the world where all classes are so intimately connected with each other as in this vast empire. . . . On the hay market of St. Petersburg we may examine the raw material out of which all Russian classes have been manufactured for centuries; and a passing glance is enough to convince us that these bearded rusty fellows are of the same race as the polished and shaven elegants whom we meet in the salons. To some extent there exists in every country a certain affinity and family likeness between the highest and lowest classes; but nowhere is this more the case than in Russia, because, contrary to the prevailing belief, in no country are the extremes of society brought into more frequent contact, and in few are the transitions from one class to another more frequent or more sudden. The peasant becomes a priest on the same day perhaps that an imperial mandate degrades the noble to a peasant, or to a Siberian colonist. Degradation to the ranks is a punishment frequently inflicted on Russian officers. . . . It requires but little polishing to convert the raw material of the muzhik into a shrewd trader; and expend but a little more pains upon this training and he will chatter away in English, French and German. . . .

In these ups and downs of fortune the lucky ones, so far as one can read, excited no general jealousy. There were outstanding serfs who won themselves reputations as actors, mechanics, or inventors, but though they could be admired they seem to have excited little competitiveness, presumably because to compete would have been to develop 'separateness'. Among the peasantry there was nothing wrong in a man's using his talent, but for another to try to emulate him for the sake of emulation and not for the sake of his own talent was something 'not done'. If a peasant bettered his land or by some unusual means succeeded in adding to it, he was bound to lose the fruits of his improvements when the Mir redistributed the land a few years later. The redistribution was a matter of traditional equity, to ensure that all took equal shares, so far as possible, of good land and bad. No one thought of it as destroying the incentives of the individual farmer; the individuality of the average serf was fully occupied in passive, cunning resistance to landowners and government agents. It was not until long after the Liberation of 1861, in the last few years before the Revolution, that most of the strips of peasant land became hereditary in tenure, and the difference between good and bad farmers began to leave some more enduring mark.

The lack of fuss about status often has a peculiar effect on Western visitors to Russia. If one comes from Britain or America, in particular, one readily receives the impression that Russians must be less egalitarian than one's own countrymen. For if the Russians accept distinction and the rewards of distinction so readily in others, it may be imagined that the mass must feel themselves inferior. But inferiority hardly enters into the picture, and if you presume on the existence of this feeling your Russian subordinates are soon going to be offended. What the Russians mostly—though not today entirely—lack is the spirit of emulation which has developed so much talent in the West. On the other hand they do not maintain the convenient fiction of the Anglo-Saxon world that all men must somehow be equally gifted, and that it is only lack of opportunity or lack of moral fibre which keeps a man from equalling the achievement of almost any other man in almost any field. The Russians, secure in their unseparateness, seem to find it easier to value men equally while at the same time admitting the inequality of their endowments. Russians do not want to be assured that a university professor is 'just a guy like themselves', because they know that he is not. And yet they believe that he has the same kind of respect for them as human beings that they have for him as a human being alongside their respect for his talents.

The Anglo-Saxon fiction is a useful one for an expanding society of individual enterprise; it causes difficulties in an industrialized society, where differences of ability between the rank and file and the managerial or technical few must force themselves on everyone's notice. The Russian fiction of equal status is convenient for a society farming on a communal basis, but less suitable for industrial life where a hierarchy of organization must somehow be established. The old tendency to work as a comradely mass has had to give way to more and more differentiation of function, and instead of breaking off to discuss with each other or with the foreman Russians have had to accept more and more of that external authority which they respect but do not love. Russian egalitarianism is a poor breeder of self-discipline, yet if only self-discipline could be more regular, authority would not need to be so arbitrary. So that the intervention of Russian authority may to a certain extent, and paradoxically, be counted evidence of the egalitarianism, though to an Englishman or American it looks uncommonly like a sign of its absence.

But there could be no greater error than to assume that in Soviet Russia nothing gets done except by dictatorship. The efficiency of the state machine depends not only on fear or on rewards, but also to a large extent on the degree to which demands can be expressed in mass forms which are familiar, which have some viable link with tradition. The tradition of equal status, for instance, has made possible a number of devices admirably suited for the Russian transition to an industrialized society, though they may strike a Westerner as naïve.

Since, for example, one can allow a man the position due to his superior talent without oneself feeling inferior in status, it follows that the man of subnormal capacities can be criticized or assisted without making him feel inferior in his turn. The English attitude is that subnormality should be glossed over as far as possible, lest the subnormal individual should feel excluded from the community, but Russians feel they can afford to single out an individual for criticism because there is no question that he still 'belongs'.

So there exist, among the many devices used to increase output, the *Doska Pochota*—the Honours Board for the best workers—and the Wall Newspaper, where the worst as well as the best are singled out for mention or caricature. In a tool factory which I visited the twist drills turned by a certain Bubnov were strung up for all to see; one could only call them passable representations of tree roots hacked out in steel. Bubnov had to submit not only to this public exhibition but also to taking part in a meeting where all the Bubnovs of the enterprise were publicly criticized, invited to confess their shortcomings, and urged to take a pledge to amend them. These forms of public criticism, to judge by the accounts of those who saw their beginnings, were to some extent spontaneous in their appearance; they certainly bear a strong flavour of the traditional practice of persuasion, confession, and readmission to the fold which existed not only in the church community but also in the peasant community. And all over Russia one sees the glass-fronted frames of the Honours Boards (sometimes, it must be said, deep in dust), where the public as well as fellow-workers may admire staring little photographs of the bonus-earning platelayers, signalmen, miners, tram conductors, barbers, cleaners, river pilots, schoolteachers, shop assistants, waiters, nurses, timber loaders . . . to the complete tale of all jobs that are not shrouded in security. Even generals and admirals may undergo an official reprimand before an audience of officers something near their own rank, while one of the army's rewards for good service is to present an officer with his photograph taken in front of the banner of his unit. Awards in industry have to be made at meetings of the whole factory, while bad workers have to sit in Chairs of Disgrace in the dining-hall, and drunkards collect their pay from Shame Booths.

My more sophisticated Moscow friends might smile at these practices, but workers with whom I have talked, especially if they came of peasant stock, regarded them as natural and desirable: 'For father to have his picture on the Board is quite something.' And the universal piecework and bonus arrangements do not run so contrary to the collective attitude as might be imagined. The man who earns the highest bonus is usually the man who 'gets on the Board', and the man who lags behind may have to bear not only the disappointment of his pay packet but also the efforts of his unit to bring him up to the norm. In schools it seems universal to arraign the backward or the misbehaved before the collective conscience of the class or the whole school; educational papers and stories for young people are full of such incidents, and the whole attitude is recommended in textbooks for the training of teachers. A recent suggestion for dealing with young people who won't work is that they should be sent away to another community *by the vote of their own*, and adults who are brought before the courts are sometimes 'remanded in the care of their workmates'.

All these practices help the Government to suppress what it calls 'bourgeois survivals of individualistic tendencies', but though the Government has encouraged and disseminated these practices they cannot in essence be called Soviet inventions. They have been developed out of the old Russian social relationships—the same relationships which have produced the Russian sense of sportsmanship, sense of humour, attitude to women, and ways of avoiding friction which, as by chance, come so near to those which English society has developed out of a very different history.

I have made much of the mass or community traditions in Russian society because they are so foreign to most Western countries, but in their essentials they are not, of course, peculiar to Russia; they are probably characteristic of the greater part of the world's population. In a rather dumb and limited fashion a solidarity of a similar kind survives among the English working class, so unnoticed by the more educated part of the nation that when Mr Richard Hoggart described it in *The Uses of Literacy* he caused something of a sensation.

Predominant though communal influences have been in Russia, however, they do not present the whole story of Russian social history. There have been at least four traditions of greater freedom which might, in favourable circumstances, have bred a stronger non-collective strain in Russians, and none of them can be regarded as extinct.

There is first the tradition of revolt—the long history of robust peasants who fled from their masters to become frontiersmen and Cossacks, the hundreds of peasant revolts, and the major risings such as those under Stenka Razin and Pugachov, which reached the dimensions of local civil war. It was the natural leaders of revolt who came to the front and largely secured the Bolshevik victory in the Civil War and War of Intervention. Many of these bold spirits became bitterly disappointed a few years later, however, and many were early victims of the purges. Revolt in ordinary civilian life seems very unlikely in Russia now, but the tradition broke out again—and to some purpose—in the strikes and rebellions inside labour camps during 1954 and 1955.

Secondly there was the religious tradition of Nil of Sorsk. A man of peasant origin and a Protestant in his generation, Nil believed that monks should remain poor, objected to using State power for religious ends, and maintained that prayer from the heart was more important than liturgical observance. He lost to the more worldly Abbot Joseph in a great fifteenth-century contest in the Russian Church, but his doctrines never ceased to appear, from time to time, through the mouths of wandering holy men. Nil was as Russian in his own way as Joseph was in his, and a priest of the Russian Church in London, Father Bloom, spoke in 1955 of the tradition of spiritual life in Russia as 'exoterically Joseph's but esoterically Nil's'. I have met two young Soviet intellectuals who returned to the faith of their fathers just because it offered an opportunity for individual choice, a justification by 'prayer from the heart'. After Nil there were many later heretical sects who might, if Russia had been politically free, have contributed something of the same element as British Nonconformists contributed to the rise of the Labour Party. Of these the Baptists retain a fair-sized membership and a number of churches in Russia, but they cannot as a community contribute to national life.

During the last decades before the Revolution independent trade was growing at a phenomenal rate. Rich merchants were buying their way into society, and some were collecting Impressionist paintings or helping to found the Moscow Art Theatre.

The lesser gentry were either improving their farming or selling their cherry orchards and mortgaging their estates to the Lopakhins whose fathers had been serfs. In the villages progressive farming, carried out by the cleverer and more ruthless peasants, was driving out the agricultural practices of the Mir. With the encouragement of the Government large numbers of peasants seized the new opportunities for enriching themselves. (Even under all the severest penalties of serfdom, and under the tyranny of landlords who harnessed serfs like dogs and recruited their daughters as concubines, the peasant liberty to trade had always remained.)

It was no wonder that the most deadly Soviet repression was directed against merchants, traders, and peasants employing labour; the possibilities for self-enrichment had formed the most powerful of the positive new strains in Russia, and the Bolsheviks were obliged to go on exploiting some of these possibilities until 1928. Lenin ejaculated on one occasion that Russia was 'the most petty-bourgeois country on the face of the earth'. This was surely untrue, yet the trading spirit of the peasants has so far proved the rock on which every Soviet policy for complete collectivization of the land has split.

Lastly there has been the great tradition of the intelligentsia, and *intelligentsia* in Tsarist Russia did not imply simply 'intellectuals', but the intellectuals who took up the noble responsibility of fighting for their fellow-Russians against tyranny and reaction. Supporters to a man of the March Revolution, the independent intelligentsia were an obvious danger to the Bolsheviks. If they were prepared not to oppose the Party line they were recruited to privileged positions, but it was clearly impossible for them to continue as an independent influence. Trotsky was still a powerful enough figure in 1929 for him to be escorted to the frontier, instead of being executed, to prevent him from preaching 'permanent revolution' inside Russia. But nine years later probably the last influence of the intelligentsia as a faction in politics was liquidated, with the execution of the clever and original Bukharin and those who shared his views.

However, many members of the old intelligentsia have survived as respected seniors, and their standards, outside politics, have had something to do with forming the standards of the younger generation. Some of the ways in which this happened, and the growth of a new intelligentsia, will be discussed in the next chapter.

6

Russian Society—The Minority

THE SUBJECT of this chapter is not the governing minority of the Soviet Union, but that much larger class of persons who earn by their occupation, their income, and their way of life a public respect which makes them the leaders of Soviet society. Members of the Soviet governing class usually enjoy similar incomes and to some extent share in the same way of life as the leaders of society, but they cannot themselves be such leaders, though a few of them may earn popular respect for their achievements and personalities. They lead lives apart from the rest of the people, and it is a matter of policy that they should do so.

The leaders of Soviet society are not a small class. They are the actors, writers, musicians, dancers, journalists, artists, architects, film and radio workers; the professors, scientists, engineers, doctors, leading technicians, and managerial personnel; they include at the top such national heroes as the pioneer pilots and Arctic explorers, and at the bottom they merge through a collection of teachers, librarians, book-keepers, and such into the less distinguished mass. Collectively they are, to use an old Soviet term, the 'specialists'.

They include the persons who seize the catalogues of new books and who if allowed will buy up within a few hours the 150,000 copies of *Gargantua and Pantagruel* announced for publication, the 20,000 copies of a brochure on foreign engines for model aeroplanes, the 75,000 copies of a translation of *Daphnis and Chloë*, the 5,000 copies of a work on the egyptologist Champollion, and the 3,000 copies of a new manual on differential equations. They include the sweating geologists, surveyors, and agronomists who fire the imagination of youth as they open up the desert or the tundra, and they include numskull 'propagandists' who make a living by publishing other people's articles over their own signature. They include genial, head-scratching young men with an unshakable conviction that their course in hydro-electrics has qualified them to build heaven upon earth, and they include sly managers and officials who cover up their embezzlement and taking of bribes with loud speeches about 'Communist duty'. They include the toiling, overloaded doctors—almost every doctor in the Soviet Union is overloaded—and they include unpleasantly smart young men and women who have got themselves jobs in third-rate orchestras, or as book-keepers in a restaurant, or as 'assistants to deputy undermanagers' so as to enjoy the opportunities for slacking and pilfering. They include internationally known names such as Kapitsa and Pasternak, and they include fussy little officials and teachers whose shallow pretensions to culture make them the biggest bores in Russia. They include enchanting actresses who would be the centre of attention (though the attention would rather embarrass them) in any Western drawing-room, and they include young vulgarians such as I once saw invading a spa hotel in the Caucasus. Swinging a decanter of vodka on the end of a string, they planted themselves in the clean white restaurant, shouting to each other in an Eastern language which seemed to require the shooting out of arms to accompany the slightest assertion. They ordered, and got, more vodka, while at surrounding tables the lady professors and doctors drew their oldfashioned skirts round them in disgust.

But without a doubt, all are specialists. They are the persons who have received some specialized education or who live by the exercise of some special gift, *not being manual operatives*. The most individual persons in Soviet society are to be found among them, and their existence as a group is acknowledged not only by their fellow-citizens but by their Government. They are in contemporary Russian 'the intelligentsia'—a term which has a much broader meaning now than it had in pre-revolutionary Russia, or than it still has in English and other languages which have borrowed it as a synonym for 'intellectuals'. To call oneself one of the intelligentsia is no great self-praise in Soviet Russia, no more than to call oneself in English a middle-class or professional person. The intelligentsia, the industrial workers, and the peasants are spoken of as the three great functional groups of the nation.

The new intelligentsia have been officially numbered. In 1937 Molotov gave the total as nine and a half millions. In 1955 Yelutin, Minister of Higher Education, estimated them in an interview with Senator Benton at 'perhaps 20 million out of 100 million workers'. It is not so easy to say who these 20 million are because Soviet statistical summaries nowadays include only 'specialists with higher or middle specialized education', i.e. persons with education from about English technical school level up to post-graduate or research standards. At the end of 1958 the total of these specialists was given as 7,476,000, and at the end of 1957 as 6,821,000. The latter figure was broken down to some extent into professions:

		% of total
Engineers (with higher education)	816,100	11·9
Technicians (with middle education)	1,257,300	18·3
Agronomists, vets, forestry, and other agricultural specialists (in all)	503,100	7·4
'Economists' and statisticians (in all)	382,600	5·6
Commercial specialists (in all)	69,500	1·0
Legal personnel (in all)	78,200	1·1
Doctors	346,000	5
Other medical personnel (with middle education), including dentists	980,300	14·3
Teachers, librarians, and similar 'cultural' workers (in all)	2,116,400	30·9
Persons in the state 'apparatus'	284,000	4·2

Important omissions from the table are people in the artistic professions, who already numbered 159,000 in 1937; scientific workers, who may from other sources be estimated at about

300,000 in research and academic work, though a fraction of them may be included under various heads above; 'book-keepers and accountants', whose numbers must have much increased since their 1,617,000 total of 1937; and most important of all, 'directors and other executives of establishments, factory departments, state farms, collective farms, etc.', who numbered 1,751,000 in 1937. (A few of these may be included above as agronomists, etc., but most of them have presumably not had specialist education.) Yelutin may have included two or three million students in his 20 million total; as for the balance, it may be partly made up of clerical workers, and it must include a good percentage of 'specialists' with limited education—the people who in the earlier Soviet years made up for their lack of academic qualification by their native intelligence and their eager desire to learn. Without them and the *ad hoc* courses they went through the First and Second Five-Year Plans could not have been carried out, and their enthusiasm helped to make Russia an exhilarating place in those years.

Since that time the pyramid of higher educational institutions has grown continuously, and by the time this book appears the basic system of education will probably have been extended to a ten-year system (including part-time education) throughout the country. It may be a long time, however, before the whole Soviet intelligentsia comes to consist, if it ever does, of people with specialized education. It will probably continue to include a fair number of persons at all levels who owe their position to their energy, organizing ability, or initiative rather than their training. In their functions, and in their relative position in the social scale, the Soviet intelligentsia are in fact much nearer to the Western ideas of a middle class than to the Western idea of an intellectual class, although their standard of living, background, and outlook are different from those of the Western middle class. The parallel partly holds even in respect of the large contingent of Western middle-class people engaged in business, since the functions of a proportion of business people as organizers and distributors must in the Soviet Union be carried out by someone, and the salaried people who carry them out count as members of the intelligentsia.

At the top the Soviet intelligentsia merge into the governing class in the person of officials too highly placed to lead an ordinary social life. It has been estimated by the Harvard researchers, Bauer, Inkeles, and Kluckhohn, that the 'ruling *élite*' consists of perhaps 10,000 persons; these people are for the most part little known to the public, their lives are organized for them, and they are rather outside what is commonly reckoned as the intelligentsia.

The highest incomes among the intelligentsia are those of a few extremely successful writers (who are paid on a royalty basis), actors, ballet-dancers, and other artists—possibly 50,000 roubles in an exceptional month. The second rank of such people probably come level with the highest officials in salary, and next below come the professors (say 4,000 to 15,000 roubles a month) and a large number of managerial people. Below this the relative positions in the salary scale are not so very different from what obtains in Britain, though there are no outstandingly high incomes such as the top lawyers, engineers, or architects may earn in the West—only good middle salaries. Teachers, apart from university teachers, are rather a depressed class as in Britain; the best manual workers earn more than they do. Doctors are an exception to the parallel; they earn about 1,400 to 1,800 roubles a month, which puts them also below the best paid manual workers. You enter the medical profession, it is felt, in a spirit of service only, the same as nurses, and the doctors (of whom about 70 per cent are women) are respected accordingly. The armed forces are a special class; the Government would be very nervous if they became too popular socially, so that although the highest officers get very large salaries, the officer class on the whole is rather kept away from the people, it does not lead the gay life of garrison towns, and does not altogether count as part of the hierarchy of salaries. The Stakhanovites and other record-breaking workers, though they earn very good money, should not be included among the Soviet intelligentsia; manual workers are rarely to be counted as leaders of Soviet society.

The concentration of a few high incomes at the top is partly reflected in savings bank deposits; according to Mr H. Schwartz, in *Russia's Soviet Economy*, 10 per cent of the depositors hold 67 per cent of all deposits above 1000 roubles. But most Russians prefer to spend rather than save, and this figure is not so significant as a Westerner might think. Though Russians are avidly buying the new goods as fast as they come into the shops, the joys of possession have not yet taken precedence over the old Russian preferences for ostentation, hospitality, and sensual self-indulgence in anything from symphony concerts down to vodka. In 1960 1,500 roubles a month was apparently considered by both manual workers and minor intellectuals as providing a reasonable standard of living. The best-paid professors may receive 15,000 roubles a month, but this does not mean that they are anything like ten times better off. They can afford to travel a good deal (though rarely outside the Soviet Union), they can buy unlimited food and drink, they may be able to buy one wooden country house (but no land), one car (if they put their names down two years or so ahead), a small selection of good clothes (again after waiting), plenty of entertainment, books, records, etc., within the censored limits, and occasional luxuries such as jewellery, furs, and Soviet scent. They can pay for some private medical attention, but this may be no better than what they would get from the regular doctor assigned to persons of such national importance. They will certainly not be able to indulge in all these things in any one year, they will have little domestic help, they will find it extremely difficult to get any repairs done, and when one weighs their privileges against the usual Soviet discomforts and inconveniences which they have to suffer, it becomes almost impossible to translate their standard of living into English terms. The prices they have to pay (in 1960), and some of the prices which the 1,500-a-month man must pay for his more modest spendings, may be illustrated from the following table, bearing in mind that people of all incomes pay only about 7 per cent of income per room for rent (including lighting and central heating), and that education at all stages is now entirely free:

Subject to being obtainable, and involving waiting from perhaps a month to (for cars) two years or more:

	Roubles
Volga car	40,000
Moskvich car	25,000
One-room prefab. house	10,000
Television set	1,750
Small refrigerator	1,500
Sewing machine	700 to 1,500
Radio set	700
Bicycle	660

Woman's coat	1,000 to 2,000 or more
Blouse and skirt	300 to 1,000
Nightdress	280
Slip	180
Man's shirt	78 to 100 or more
Women's stockings	18 to 40
Tea or coffee set of good design	150, 250 or more

Always available (apart from seasonal fruits):

Bread	0.50 per lb.
Potatoes	0.45 per lb.
Butter	10.65 per lb.
Cheese	11.80 per lb.
Fresh meat (badly hacked)	4.60 to 8.20 per lb.
Best Georgian tea	34.20 per lb.
Oranges (in May)	6.35 per lb.
Strawberries (in May)	13.60 per lb.
Wine	18 to 25 per bottle
Brandy	40 per bottle
2-lb. box of chocolates	82

Petrol	3.40 or 4.15 per gallon

Very good restaurant meal, including drinks, perhaps	100 or more
Restaurant meal of 2 dishes and a little drink	20 to 30
Canteen or popular restaurant meal	5 to 10

These are the figures of early 1960, but part of the difficulty of estimating Soviet standards of living is that prices are liable to change at any time as the Government operates the turnover tax which is the major source of Soviet revenue. This tax is not levied at a flat rate on all commodities; the prices of bare necessities and public services have always been kept low, while the prices of other necessities such as sugar or butter, or of semi-luxury and luxury articles, have fluctuated widely accordingly to the quantities available and the extent to which the Government wished to soak up purchasing power. Prices of manufactured goods have been cut repeatedly as they became more plentiful; a bicycle in 1959 cost little more than a third of what it did in 1951. The price of a restaurant meal in a Moscow hotel went up by about ten times during the war and has fallen by about eight times since. The price of vodka has been almost doubled during the last few years as part of the campaign against drunkenness.

Prices as a whole will almost certainly continue to fall. They are too fluid in general for money to be a satisfactory index of the question which fascinates foreigners perhaps too much—whether there is a 'privileged class' in the Soviet Union. Industrial workers and peasants, as well as intelligentsia, are queuing for the new consumer goods, and when they give way to a Russian spend-thrift feeling they may use the best restaurants too. One night in the Baku restaurant I shared a table with a shoe operative, a cook, and a typist who were spending at least 70 roubles a head, and at lunch next day in the Artistic Café, opposite the Moscow Art Theatre, I sat with a shock-haired lorry-driver who was spending 22 roubles out of his monthly 1,200 on fresh caviar, ham and eggs, and a quarter of a pint of brandy.

As goods become more plentiful, and rationing by the purse is less necessary, not only prices but salaries are being adjusted. In 1959 many of the highest salaries were being cut by half— I heard of academic salaries reduced from 20,000 to 10,000 roubles a month. At the same time the lowest salaries—perhaps 400 roubles a month for the lowest unskilled work—are being raised by stages until in 1965 they are to be doubled.

It is open to any Soviet citizen to earn extra money in his spare time, though the limits are narrow. Many people give private lessons—in foreign languages, mathematics, physics, typewriting —advertising themselves through the Moscow City advertisement panels. Lawyers and doctors are allowed some private practice, if they can find clients or patients, and some doctors put up little enamel plates to advertise their speciality— 'Sexual Weakness', for instance. Workmen also find a ready private market for their skill, since one of the greatest bottlenecks in Soviet life is the matter of repairs. (In 1959, according to the Soviet press, it was taking three to four months to get one's shoes repaired, and the Government was planning to set up during the next three years 29,000 enterprises for 'individual shoemaking' and repair, 22,000 for dressmaking and repair of clothing, and 12,100 for servicing household articles.) Until recently the difficulty for the workman has been to get hold of the materials. From reported cases we know how timber, paint, tiles, cloth, leather, etc., have been diverted from public use to private repairs, and some directors of factories have not been above organizing this kind of thing on a large scale. But there is no bar to selling one's skill or talents privately, so long as the materials are honestly come by. The Government advertises for people to add to their income in their spare time by acting as agents for government insurances, which can be taken out on one's 'house, furniture, clothing, car, cart, horse, cow, camel, or donkey'. Sub-letting of houses or flats is also legal, but buying in order to sell at a profit constitutes the serious crime of 'speculation'. Otherwise it has always been legal for Soviet citizens to make what they could out of the small opportunities allowed them for private enterprise. It is not advisable, however, to make too much money in this way, or you will be likely to receive a visit from the Finance Section of the MVD, and even if they are satisfied that you have kept within the law you may find yourself making a 'voluntary' contribution to State funds—a million roubles was the figure in the case of one or two peasants who used wartime opportunities to enrich themselves. There is no prospect of the very small sector of private enterprise becoming a national problem; if it did the Government would probably deal with it by a currency reform. As it is, the opportunities provide one of the useful safety-valves in Soviet life, but I doubt very much if they are by themselves an incentive for anyone to want to raise himself from the working class to the intelligentsia.

However, there are other distinctions inevitably felt by everybody between the lives led by the intelligentsia and the lives of other Soviet citizens. There are no such contrasts between luxury and beggary as in for example Persia; there is no very brilliant social round for people at the top or for their children who sometimes live without working, nor are their private lives illustrated in *Ogonyok* or any other magazine. But there is, in the first place, a natural distinction in dress between the blackcoated and the manual worker. In plays about contemporary life—and all plays are subject to a stiff censorship—those who belong to the intelligentsia dress better than workers, the men often much better, in suits which the West would recognize as of good middle-class quality. In Soviet caricatures the practical working man who exposes the pretensions of some idle 'specialist' always wears a cap, while the middle-class man is shown with a hat, cigarette-holder, ostentatious handkerchief, and similar gear. According to no less an authority than Molotov, distinctions in dress appear to be a matter of course. For when the British Military Attaché, Major-General Hilton, was arrested during a country walk in Russian clothes on suspicion of being a spy, Molotov sought to excuse the police on the grounds that 'in his outward appearance the General did not at all resemble a cultured person, but was dressed as an ordinary worker'. A large and impressive-looking Irish friend of mine visited Moscow in 1957 and insisted on exploring by himself though he spoke no Russian. When he became hungry he managed to buy himself a sandwich and a beer at a dingy stall surrounded by men in greasy working clothes. Their looks made it clear that he was not welcome at their stall and when he pretended not to understand one of them who spoke a little English took him by the lapel and said 'Coat too good!' (The Irish have a good deal in common with the Russians, however, and the situation was dissolved by the Irishman turning his coat inside out and continuing his meal while wearing it so.)

A confirmation of these distinctions is to be found in that peculiar phenomenon, Soviet advertising. There is a certain amount of *commerchesky* or 'commercial' advertising of goods and services in the Soviet Union, and the men who are depicted buying cigarettes or ice-cream, or putting their money away in the savings-bank, always wear the best sort of Soviet clothes, while many of them will wear soft hats instead of caps. Their radiant wives are neater than most Soviet wives can manage to be, their flats are enviably large and uncluttered, and their children, shining with good health as they eat their breakfast cereal, are well above even the high Soviet average of presentability. Some of these families, it would appear, may inhabit a small house with a garden. In another advertisement a young couple are waiting beside the Aeroflot machine which is to fly them to their holiday by the Black Sea; their fluttering scarves, their overcoats and their luggage are again of high Soviet quality. When I discussed these idealizations with the more propagandist Russians they defended them as being 'more cultured', but a free-lance artist simply said: 'The public prefer not to see pictures of persons wearing clothes as poor as their own.' She added that the idea of prosperity (even then, in 1945) was something she found it necessary to exploit when she was asking for work: 'You wear your best clothes, of course, when you go to see the factory director, you act as though you didn't really need the job of doing his posters and decorations, you offer him a Troika cigarette (the most expensive Soviet brand), and when you come away *you casually leave the box on the table*!'

Besides their better clothing the intelligentsia also enjoy, and openly, some privilege in housing accommodation. Very large numbers—possibly millions—of technicians, doctors, teachers, and the like must still bring up their families on the usual Soviet ration of a single room, but if any family has more than a single room it will probably be the family of a member of the intelligentsia, a high officer or official, or one of the outstanding manual workers. It has been officially recognized that writers, artists, and officers of high rank are entitled to 'additional accommodation', i.e. a second room. A great many of the intelligentsia, too, are among those who own a country shack or *dacha*. The average *dacha* is about the size of a large greenhouse and not much more substantial; it is unfit for habitation in winter and is unlikely to have electricity, gas, or running water. The total amenities of *dacha* and town apartment together, including the *dacha* garden, will rarely amount to as much as those of a typical three-bedroom dwelling on an English housing estate, but the chance to camp out in a summer *dacha* is much prized, and once again an official statement has been made: the possession of a *dacha* as well as a town dwelling is acknowledged to 'promote the creative concentration of mental forces'.

I noticed a somewhat similar distinction when visiting a porcelain factory at Leningrad; the large rooms where workers carried out routine decorations had music from a loudspeaker, while the little rooms where the designers worked were left quiet.

On the other hand persons who have received a university or higher education may expect, in principle, to be directed to their first job, unlike millions of humbler Russians, and to be directed probably to one of the distant and least developed parts of the Soviet Union. But to judge by the ceaseless stream of cartoons and sketches on the subject of *fils à papa* who manage to get directed to Moscow or some other big city, and the regular complaints of understaffing in distant provinces, this regulation is circumvented by many.

The crucial element in class distinction, however, would seem to consist less in the distribution of privileges than in the attitude taken up by the privileged to the under-privileged, or by the under-privileged to the privileged. Foreigners are usually shocked at some of the Soviet distinctions which depend upon rank—the special waiting-rooms and wicket-gates for persons of standing, and the seats reserved at the theatre for the highest officers and officials, who may be admitted, unlike everyone else, after the curtain has gone up. If you occupy one of these reserved seats by mistake you may pass as a person of suitable rank if your clothes are good enough and your bearing appropriate. A good many minor distinctions depend upon clothes, as on the occasion when I was startled to find myself singled out of a crowd of peasants waiting to board a train, and beckoned by the conductress into the carriage reserved for 'Mothers and Children', where I spent the journey in the company of four mothers, two children, and twenty-six empty seats. Privileges for 'specialists' have been familiar since the early days of the Revolution, when many of them received double the ordinary rations of food, and Lenin ordered four times the ration to be issued to the physiologist Pavlov and his family. During the war it was thought natural that leading young actors and ballet-dancers should be exempt from military service; for the British not to exempt theirs appeared to Russians not more 'democratic' or egalitarian but merely silly.

Privileges such as these do not excite so much resentment in Russia as they would in Britain or many other countries, largely because they are felt to depend on 'horizontal' distinctions of function, though foreigners with their sharper sense of place would regard them more as 'vertical' distinctions of grade. In factories, my Russian friends tell me, 'the workers speak roughly to the director because they are workers, and the director speaks roughly back, in order to show that he is the same sort of man as them'. Apparently he finds this a more successful method than resorting to the regulation which lays it down that 'Orders of the director of the factory are unconditionally binding on all personnel'.

However, some people do presume upon the advantages which their positions give them, and there is indeed a coarse parvenu element in the Soviet middle class—characters who resemble the *nouveaux riches* of Balzac, as one of my Moscow friends used to say, except that it is power and position, not commerce, which has made them so. Russians are not usually at home with self-assertion, and elevation above one's fellows understandably brings out un-Russian traits such as rudeness to waiters or disdain for peasants, in some. One's position can often be more insisted on in leisure or domestic life than at work, and since there is still a good deal of 'privilege' rationing—almost all the seats in the Bolshoi Theatre are allotted by privilege—the Soviet middle class includes a lot of people who are somewhat too proud of being able to get priority for theatre, ballet, and concert tickets, for sleeper berths, air passages, or newly-arrived goods in the shops, and who will abuse the privileges and even the funds of their unit to get these things. (Other citizens, however, often find that the most effective title to priority is a hundred-rouble note.) Some of the wives of the 'arrived' exhibit personalities as artificial, tense, and gaudy as the tight silk dresses which fail to disguise their overfed peasant figures, but there are plenty of others who preserve their native peasant goodness as naturally as they wear their more comfortable clothes. At a more sophisticated level there is the hard, brilliant exterior of, say, Mrs X., whom both foreigners and Russians find insufferable in her consciousness of her position as an actress, of her husband's position as a playwright, and of the fact that she is one of the few Soviet women who might by her elegance of dress, coiffure, and carriage be taken for a foreigner. But for every Mrs X. one could find more than one in the same class as, for example, the petite, delicately-made, home-keeping Mrs Shostakovitch, a lady of such unspoilt charm and sincerity that one could hardly think of a more melting ambassadress for her nation.

But although position in Soviet society may breed parvenu manners in many individuals, there are several good reasons why such manners have not become and are not very likely to become characteristic of the new middle class.

There is first simply the old communal atmosphere in which nearly everyone is reared. Some young Russians may seem alarmingly modern in their neat suits, technical vocabularies, and their rather brusque style of conversation, yet when they stumble at some social uneasiness or ignorance they will probably smile engagingly and fall back on the egalitarian good nature to which they were brought up. There are others who cover up their embarrassment with a crude defiance or a 'Why should I?' attitude; these seem usually to be the children of over-indulgent parents who, living perhaps in well-to-do semi-isolation, 'didn't want them to have such a hard time as we had ourselves'. But this kind of isolation from the general atmosphere is difficult to attain, and all the weight of nursery schools and every other kind of school is against it. Lazy and drunken adolescents form a well-recognized problem in Soviet Russia, but their attitude, even if persisted in, is not going to be a dominating influence in society.

Secondly there is the very widely felt respect for all that is described by the magic word *kulturny*—education, culture in the Western sense, cleanliness, neatness, helpfulness, punctuality, and considerate behaviour in general. To accuse someone of being 'uncultured' (*nekulturny*) is not a light matter, and the word is heard among industrial workers as well as the intelligentsia; it may signify that you do not clean your teeth, that you never read a book, or that you are pushing rudely or giving way to a coarse expression of opinion. Partly because of the general urge towards education and culture, and partly because of a shortage of light reading, the Soviet people, as may be judged by what they read in trains or buses, are one of the most studious nations in the world. A philistine reaction against culture or things of the intellect is one of the last things likely to happen in Russia, and thus the intelligentsia have less reason to feel a class superiority because of their interests and abilities. 'Specialism' is felt to be something open to almost everybody; in the lightest of contemporary comedies (Mikhalkov's *Dikari*) a diplomat and a vet, on a camping holiday by the Black Sea, take up with a police girl and a female lion-tamer, also camping, without the slightest hint that there is anything but a functional distinction in the status of any of them.

After spending a little time in Russia one is bound to make the pleasant discovery that the growth of parvenu traits is modified, as in other countries, by the surviving cultural traditions of the old aristocracy, the old intelligentsia, and the old middle class. For in spite of the Revolution, the emigration, and the purges, there remains a fair number of former members of these classes in positions of some importance, and a much larger number of their children, now in their thirties or forties, who were brought up as far as possible in the traditions of their kind through all the agonies of the years after 1917. These persons are almost always in 'specialist' jobs, though rarely among those specialists— scientific administrators, etc.—who count as members of the governing class. They include academics of all kinds, translators who learned their excellent English or French in an old-fashioned home, some doctors or teachers, quite a few technologists, and naturally a high proportion of people in the artistic professions. I heard of two persons in modest middle-class jobs whose parents were among the Percys and Cecils of Tsarist Russia—families once so powerful and internationally famous that for the sake of their descendants it would probably be safer not to mention the names here.

The time is long past when persons such as these, and their traditions, could survive only surreptitiously. For the very reason that no factions can be permitted in a totalitarian state, it has been necessary for the Revolution to take over and absorb into itself, where it has not killed off, the traditions of the former privileged classes. The remnants of these classes could not be permitted to turn their backs on all public life and withdraw into noncooperation as the French aristocracy did under the Republic. They have been used in positions for which their education or talents qualified them, and their group existence, though officially denied them, has been able to persist in private life in a modified form, partly because most of them are to be found in a comparatively limited number of professions. It is reported that these families remain anxious about the possibility of educating their children, under Soviet conditions, in the way that they would wish, but the fact remains that so long as they keep to themselves and observe the decencies of Soviet flat life they can and do continue to give their children, and their children continue to pass on to the third generation, a home background and a home education different from the usual.

As the crude political contrasts of early Soviet days were replaced by a stress on the feeling of continuity and of nationalism it became the done thing to admire older architecture, classical literature, even mediaeval church art; it has also become the done thing to admire the older, more courtly manners (though they are not officially called 'older') instead of the brusque and raw behaviour which was typical of Soviet society in its first years. The respect for older traditions received a further fillip during the war, when the Tsarist generals of the Napoleonic Wars and the First World War were elevated into national heroes. A surviving Tsarist Officer, General Ignatiev, was deputed, just as the war was ending, to impress on the new generation of military cadets his six feet six of old-fashioned courtliness and charm. At the same time a school for diplomats (privately admitted to be much needed) was opened, where aspirants have since received not only political education but instruction in international codes of manners, dress, and food.

Persons of the former privileged classes, or their descendants, who have survived until the 1960's are naturally people who have learned how to keep out of political trouble; there is no taboo against them any more, and prejudice against their origins has been giving way to downright curiosity for many years. Among younger Russians of sensibility there is such respect for age in itself, and such admiration for the greater delicacy and finish of old-fashioned manners, or even of old-fashioned ways of speech, that the influence of this surviving minority permeates far into society. It spreads through personal contact in the first place, and more widely through the influence of stage and screen, where in contemporary dramas the assumed ideal of good manners is a blend of peasant courtesy and good nature with the forbearance, dignity, and capacity for intimacy of the older tradition, instead of the rough, pushing manners of the street which were more acceptable in the 1920's. The old Petersburg manner has spread well beyond the confines of the old capital, and among some of the young as well as their seniors. It is a magnificent blend of dignity and ease. If some international television organization were to institute a competition for the discovery of what they would probably call 'Sir World'—the man most distinguished by ease and charm of manner, dignity, presence, forbearance, and other attributes of a gentleman—a good competitor from Leningrad would run neck and neck with the best that British public schools can produce.

What has not been permitted to survive in Soviet Russia is any of the class attitude which went with the older manners. The mass of Russians would not now tolerate it for a moment, whatever they may think of the new functional distinctions, and the remaining representatives of the old upper classes are naturally those who have been able to feel, or at least to feign, a proper Russian egalitarianism. Some of the new intelligentsia might take up attitudes of condescension, at first perhaps unconsciously, but it takes two to make a condescension, and you would have to look far for remnants of old-fashioned submissiveness today. You might still discover, in charge of the toilet arrangements of some hotel or restaurant, one of those tall, bearded old servants who rises to his feet with dignity and remains standing while you wash, with the hand towel presented across his outstretched arms. But one should not mistake for an attitude of subservience the wheedling manner which Russians so often adopt when trying to persuade a functional superior of something; if you watch you will find that they can use the same manner in trying to persuade someone who is functionally their equal or their subordinate.

Class distinctions based on birth or breeding instead of function are so foreign to Soviet society that Soviet refugees coming to the West are shocked to meet with them, for the first time in their lives, among some of the refugees of the 1917 period. One Soviet refugee who has made himself a successful life in Britain has described to me how on a holiday in Spain he had a difference of opinion with an ex-Tsarist general, an earlier refugee, over the right way to address the Spaniard who was cleaning his shoes. 'Why do you call that man "Señor"?' said the general; 'he is only a bootblack.' 'But everyone in Spain is "Señor", and to me the bootblack is "Señor" too!'

In spite, however, of all the influences which may soften Soviet class distinctions, the lives led by the intelligentsia continue to appear more individual and interesting than those of manual workers; they command more social respect and usually (though not necessarily) more money, and they provide greater opportunities for those who want to indulge a taste for power, a finer sensibility, or a taste for solitude. Jobs which mean dirty hands, as one may gather from the editorial comments of *Komsomolskaya Pravda*, are beginning to be regarded as a 'lower' affair, and in Dudintsev's novel one well-qualified engineer says to another: 'Why on earth mess about with all that rust? Flirting with the working class, I see!' The children of the intelligentsia expect to be able to earn themselves the same standard of living as their parents enjoy, and Mr Khrushchev complained in 1958 that only 30-40 per cent of Moscow University students were children of workers or peasants; some students, he asserted, were getting to the university through parental influence. The fact is that, now that most children are staying at school until they are 17, it has become increasingly difficult to induce a sufficient proportion of them to take up manual work.

Direction of labour has been tried before, with poor results. The present situation is being dealt with by striking new decrees, along with a lot of persuasion and propaganda to show the attractions and social significance of manual occupations. Under the new decrees schoolchildren from 14 to 17 are now supposed to engage in part-time work provided they have reached a minimum standard of education, and at 17, if they wish to enter the university or other higher institution, they must first work for two years at some job related to the studies they hope to take up, attending evening classes in these at the same time. (I met an aspiring young biochemist who had been accepted in a laboratory where she was to do blood tests and similar work for two years.) The authorities perhaps hope that some young people may tire of the double burden and give up their idea of entering the university. There is no doubt that these measures are meant seriously; students already in the universities are included retrospectively,

I was told, and after qualifying they will have to do two years' work in a lower grade before they can take up employment of a graduate standard. As to the younger pupils, it will be a long time before every school in the Soviet Union has organized satisfactory part-time work or links with local industry; there have been campaigns to this end before, but if the present one is eventually successful, educationists from all over the world will be flocking to study the Soviet solution of this problem which faces us all.

The intelligentsia are thus a body of citizens, perhaps more than 20 million in number, whose social characteristics (apart from their functions) are still in a fluid and transitional state. It is impossible to say whether they will eventually be accepted as a privileged class or whether, with the raising of the standard of living all round, they will be integrated, as a merely more interesting group, into a kind of community not yet seen in any country. What happens will depend, as usual, partly on the Soviet Government and partly on the reactions of the Soviet people.

Meanwhile, what seems important is not so much the existence of this minority as a class, but the fact that 20 million individuals have had the opportunity of at least a limited amount of personal development. It is perhaps paradoxical that the Soviet régime, usually respected and feared abroad for its monolithic solidarity, should have provided some of its own people with such scope.

I have spoken of the intelligentsia as the Minority because although most of them retain some of the old mass loyalties, their influence in Soviet society is all in the direction of differentiation. They present to the mass of the people not merely the picture of a group with enviable privileges; they present *models* of a thousand kinds for individual Russians, and models have been sadly lacking through most of Russian history. The old Russian village offered all its variety of human nature without much emphasis on types; you could be what you liked so long as you fitted into the community, but there were few models to give you an idea of what you might in fact be. The new Russia offers models for every sort of gift of intellect, manual skill, or sensibility, even to some extent models for different kinds of temperament—the daring, the obsessive, the amusing, the self-sacrificing. . . . Individuals who might in the old days have been one of the followers of Nil or of the sects can find a vocation as teachers, maybe, or *feldshers* (medical assistants) in pioneering parts of the country; there is perhaps even a vocation for vanity in the few dress houses, where the mannequins, who used to be just embarrassed Russian girls who happened to be pretty, are nowadays beginning to look more professional.

It is still rarely possible to tell who Russians are or what they do by their appearance or bearing. Apart from the entertainment professions and to some extent the Services they are not much concerned with showing what they are. In the porcelain factory young men painting china may look as though they should be sailors or labourers; in the art galleries the students copying masterpieces may look like barbers' boys, while young male shop assistants may look as clearcut as scientists should do. An evening in central Moscow's cafés, restaurants, and theatre foyers gives one a mere medley of impressions—'successful' types like the cruder Italian businessmen, tall, composed young Leningraders, mousey women with neat heads, watered-down Chaliapins who look as though they are making a good thing out of the system, engaging little Armenians, fat, clay-complexioned wives, surgeons larking like schoolboys, bearded old academicians, 'Alphonse' types of Edwardian young face, tarted-up but embarrassed young misses being proudly taken out by young men who would in London count as street-traders, leonine grey intellectuals, officers swollen with wine, students sardonically surveying the whole scene, and at a table by the door an old peasant with flat cap, piggy eyes, huge beard and Russian boots, shyly sipping tea. Except for the peasant and the officers in uniform it is impossible to tell what jobs any of them might be in. Some of them are certainly manual workers.

The time to draw a character sketch of the Soviet 'middle class has not yet arrived. But one must wonder whether a very significant part is not going to be played by the increased liberty and opportunities for individual development which Russian women, like women in other industrialized societies, are beginning to enjoy. Already one sees a few young women in Moscow or Leningrad or Kiev whose bearing is neither that of the traditionally reserved mass nor that of the flaunting few; they are unembarrassedly conscious of the pleasant appearance they have been able to contrive, and they present an awareness of their own self-respect which is something new. One may doubt—because of their bearing even more than their clothes—whether they are Russians or foreigners, until one hears them speak. A good many Russian men are obviously going to compete for such women. And whether they marry such women or the more retiring types who form the majority, they are more and more often going to get two- or three-room flats where housepride and pride in possessions will come more naturally than in the old higgledy-piggledy single room. It is too soon to say how far these new qualities may develop: the official attitude, with its new emphasis on formal wedding ceremonies and so forth is all in favour of stable home life, but it is also much worried by the Russian tendency to spoil children in the comparative isolation of these new homes. However, indications of the future are more to be looked for in such families than in the more violent phenomena of *stilyagi*, illegal trading, or occasional student unrest.

'Individuality *had* to break out in all directions after all the years of repression', said an intelligent young student to me. He went on to insist that the apparently violent outbreaks and the widespread rudeness are never quite so violent or rude as foreigners seem to think. The rudeness is not usually an assertion against all comers, it is not even the bluntness of a Yorkshireman; it springs rather from the feeling that 'We're all in it together—why should I consider you or you me?' Except perhaps for certain very maladjusted characters the rudeness still has roots in the solidity of the mass; it exists partly because of those roots.

7

Manners, Morals, and Taste

WHEN A foreigner takes his first plunge into Russian life, away from Intourist guides and goodhearted hotel waitresses, his first impression of Russian manners may well be that they are rough or almost non-existent.

Gathering up his Russian words and his fifty kopecks, he is about to speak at the little Metro booking-office window when a rough arm thrusts past him and through the window up to the elbow, pushing a crumpled rouble into the hand of the old woman at the ticket-machine. 'Two!' grunts the rough arm, obviously in a hurry. Everyone else seems to be in a hurry too, the window is very small, and rough hand after rough hand pushes through until the foreigner realizes that he will never be served with a ticket during the rush hour until he too thrusts in his hand without respect for other hands. He endures the crush in the Metro train—he has heard of that before—and emerging thankfully into the street, crosses carefully between the pedestrian studs. The Soviet highway code is strict, yet buses, lorries and cars bear down on him as though the crossing did not exist, and he skips on to the pavement, where he has to look out sharply for other people, for they will not look out much for him. Younger people may stop him, recognizing him as a foreigner, and may speak with a remarkable brusqueness, though no unpleasant intent, asking intelligent questions perhaps and then turning away without a greeting.

The surface impression of Russian city manners is bound to be a poor one, and it contrasts with the gentle warmth and disarming courtesy which Russians nearly always show when they enter into anything which could qualify as even a passing relationship. In crowds they generally appear reserved, offhand, sunk in themselves. They are not one of the nations irresistibly impelled to talk in trains; when they talk they can talk endlessly, but they can also stay monosyllabic and glum. They have a natural tendency to use no more energy, no more faculties, than are required for what they have in hand at the moment. In 1959 I went to the Soviet Army Theatre for a performance of Zorin's *Good Fellows*, a new play at that time, and one of the most light-hearted comedies ever seen in Russia. The relaxation of police control was already several years old, yet when I looked at the Saturday night audience before the curtain went up I found it almost impossible, even after twenty-five years acquaintance with Russians, to believe that this wooden-faced, uninteresting crowd would light up—as they very soon did—and become a receptive, hilarious public for the play.

Some of the brusqueness in contemporary Russia is new, but the contrast between superficial appearances and more personal relationships is an old one. It was found striking 120 years ago by the German traveller Kohl, who said:

Englishmen are too apt to attribute the courtesy of the Russians to a slavish disposition, but the courteous manner in which two Russian peasants are sure to salute each other when they meet cannot be the result of fear engendered by social tyranny. On the contrary, a spirit of genuine politeness pervades all classes, the highest as well as the lowest.

The old communal ways are still the most powerful element in Soviet manners and morals. They show themselves vigorously, for example, in that most spontaneous and recent Soviet development, the sense of sportsmanship. The State provides grounds and facilities for clubs, but the enthusiasm comes from the people, and it is a very recent enthusiasm. It received an official fillip when the Soviet Government sent the *Dinamo* team on their victorious tour of Britain; Moscow residents say it was only after this tour that small boys began to make a habit of kicking a ball or a bundle of rags around the backyards.

Organized sport and athletics have made a tremendous outlet for the vitality and 'aggression' of Russian players and spectators, but the old feelings of solidarity, of decent relations between man and man, seem to have prevented any development of the dirty play and ugly crowd behaviour typical of so many countries where sport is a new thing. Soviet international teams have sometimes made a bad impression through being overzealous about national prestige, but I do not think foreigners have ever had to complain of any lack of sportsmanship on the field. When foreign teams or athletes defeat Russians on Russian ground they never meet with unpleasantness from the crowd unless they have been thought unsporting; the crowds respect the victors and vent their feelings by booing their own side. In domestic matches Soviet crowds are noisily partisan, and Soviet star players sometimes get too big for their boots. The police would step in if crowds showed a tendency to get as rough as the roughest British football crowds, and spoiled star players can be officially penalized in a way which would never happen in Britain, yet the sportsmanship of the Russian crowd and of the average Russian player is too natural to be the result of official discipline.

However, the widespread and healthy survival of old standards is clearly not the only influence in forming Soviet *mores*. The State has intervened continuously in the field of manners and morals, partly in the attempt to form 'Soviet man', but even more because the chaos, confusion, and crime resulting from the Revolution, the Civil War, the industrialization, and the purges made intervention inevitable. There was a brief period when the new State encouraged children to report on their parents' 'counter-revolutionary activities', and free love was regarded as 'a blow to the bourgeois conception of the family', but in 1928 the First Five-Year Plan put an end to all that.

Since those days the official attitude has been serious, very often solemn, and in general what countries further West would call solid and old-fashioned. It has been expressed not only through regulations but through schools, parents' meetings, and the Komsomol (the Young Communist organization), through discussion in the press, in trade unions and factory units, and through the non-penal activities of the ordinary police (the 'militia') as well as through films and novels and plays. The public have mostly met official enterprise with earnest interest and they have given the authorities a great deal of co-operation in this field, often taking the initiative themselves. The official attitude, in fact, has largely counted for its support on the Russian care for communal standards; it is an attitude itself partly rooted in that care. The Russian spirit is not offended when private persons take it upon themselves to persuade individuals back into line with accepted behaviour, and you have not to be long in Russia before you may see people quietly remonstrating with rude boys, boorish adults, noisy youths, or urchins who have climbed over the fence so as to see a show without paying. Since 1959 volunteers who are willing to deal with breaches of public manners by methods of persuasion have been formed into a *Druzhina*, or 'Company', with red armlets.

Most Russians needed little encouragement to return to the idea of a stable family life—if indeed they had ever given it up during the early days of the Revolution. They are not a promiscuous people, and illicit unions are often as stable as the registered ones. During the worst years which came later many spoke of family life as 'the only bit of the world you can have to yourself'. But campaigns about morals and manners have not only been concerned with such fundamental matters, and it is typical of Soviet Russia that minor points of behaviour have been treated with equal seriousness. Town habits had to be inculcated in the mass of city-dwellers, whose peasant-born good nature turned to bluntness or apathy in a life where they were herded together, overpoliced, overdisciplined, and for so long almost without leisure. Simple necessary habits of hygiene, tidiness, and self-discipline, restrictions on jaywalking, smoking, or spitting have been treated with the same polite strictness as respect for elders or for women. And attitudes which to a foreigner may appear solemn often miss being priggish in practice, because of the comfortable warmth of the community. This is particularly so in the training of the young. A collection of lectures on *The Home Training of Children* (published in Leningrad in 1959) deals with the following themes among others:

Before going to school at seven years of age, children should be used to obeying necessary orders.

Children should always show respect to elders or superiors, greeting them formally and face-to-face.

Children should help with the housework. (Instance where the Komsomol and Pioneer organization of a school persuaded all children to do so, and received the thanks of several parents.)

At table one should remove the spoon from the cup before drinking. Bones, etc., should be deposited on the plate, never beside it.

The well-to-do must see that their children enjoy no obviously privileged position. (Instance of the manager of an important factory who would never take his son to school in his car.)

Parents should take serious interest in their children's studies but should not make things too easy for them.

'What will people say?' is a base motive compared with duty to the community or to one's neighbour.

Modesty and simplicity are marks of the highest culture; children should not be praised too much nor allowed to show off.

The effects of such precepts as these, it need hardly be said, are far from being fully realized in Soviet life, but it would be wrong to imagine that Russians feel them to be priggish, or that the only force behind them is that which stems from school-masters, officials, or police. The bringing up of children is as common a theme of conversation in Russia as anywhere else.

The warmth of old-fashioned communal approval is naturally not always enough to satisfy the more original or more sensitive, especially among the young. Many have of their own accord taken up some of the manners of pre-revolutionary Russia—manners typical of the aristocracy rather than the old bourgeoisie. The stagy or romantic flavour is often the attraction; some young men sport Pushkinesque side-burns and affect the manner of a nineteenth-century Guardsman, flinging about such phrases as 'Devilish good' and twirling their moustaches if they have them. The dignified contrast of older manners attracts others; at the opera or in the best holiday hotels it is not uncommon to see men, by no means elderly, who greet a lady with old-fashioned bows and kissing of the hand. No doubt some of these manners were originally adopted by way of protest, but the authorities do not now seem to frown on even the most formal revivals unless someone suggests that old codes of manners are a necessary guide for Soviet society. This is inadmissible, but suitable examples from pre-revolutionary Russia may be cited for emulation. The Leningrad handbook on the training of children quoted with approval, under the heading 'Training is Everything', the *mot* of the old actress Sumbatova-Yuzhina, who always rose to greet her guests in spite of age and infirmity, remarking when they pressed her to sit down: 'It's not me that's standing up—it's my training.'

Revivals of Tsarist manners must seem to the Government more desirable than the aping of 'American' ways among the rougher, well-to-do youths of whom so much has been heard abroad. It is only fair to say that *stilyagi* in Moscow are far less in evidence than teddy boys are in London, and their loutishness seems to be 'American' only in form. You may be allowed to call it Russian loutishness so long as you add something about 'bourgeois survivals', and at least the youth committees and similar bodies seem prepared to deal with each *stilyag* as an individual Russian rather than as part of an 'American' problem.

Some foreign influences, apparently, are beginning to be regarded as worthy of imitation. It was quite startling in 1959 to find a newly-published reference book describing the British as models of considerate public behaviour:

The civilized character of the working people of England shows itself in their self-discipline and the way they behave among themselves. . . . In other European countries one can see people rude to each other when they accidentally collide; in England it passes off with 'Excuse me' and 'Sorry' and 'My fault'. . . . The visitor sees people of an age-old culture who, not through any commands from above but through their own inward impulses are polite, conscious of their own human dignity, and respectful of others' individuality.

At the same time I was told of sophisticated Soviet circles—admirers probably of *The Forsyte Saga*, so widely read in Russia—whose ideal of behaviour and bearing is that of the English *dzhentelman*.

In general the relaxation of political control has released more spontaneity in public manners. People seem more relaxed, a little more apart from each other than they used to do; one might say that they do not seem to need the mass quite as much as formerly. Crowds in Moscow may not appear very considerate but they are a good deal more so than they were earlier, when people wearily sank themselves into the mass and just pushed.

Meanwhile, the concepts of being moral, considerate, quiet, cultured, tidy, clean, well-read, respectful, reasonable, and so forth have all rather fused in the public mind into one general but somewhat fluid picture—that of the 'cultured' (*kulturny*) man or woman. Breaches of good order, manners, and morals are characterized by the word which has become well known in the West—*nekulturny* (uncultured)—though I have the impression that it is somewhat less used, and more damning when used, than it used to be. The imported word 'hooligan' has almost as wide an application. Small boys who drop ice-cream papers may be 'hooligans'; so are noisy, shouting fourteen-year-olds, and so were the adolescent gangs who used to knife people in order to steal their clothing. One Sunday during the war I found a wooden cross over a fresh grave in Dyakovo churchyard, just outside Moscow, inscribed pathetically by hand: 'In Memory of My Husband, Who Died At The Hands of Hooligans.' A few days later I passed a woman who was trying to quieten the squalling twins whom she was carrying one on each arm: 'Come on now! Be quiet!' she said, and suddenly invented a word: 'Stop hooliganating!' (*Dovolno huliganovat!*)

The scene is full of contrasts in all conscience. One or two hotels maintain American standards of cleanliness, but hotels less visited by foreigners, especially in the provinces, can be nauseating. In city streets there really is no litter; litter-bin-cum-spittoons are set up every twenty yards or so, and people have been trained to use them. But lavatories are another thing. Public ones are as discreetly concealed as in New York, but with this concealment the resemblance abruptly ends. Cubicles, doors, or partitions are most often non-existent, even in many hotels, and elsewhere the foreigner may find it impossible to stomach these places at all. Back in 1934 one sometimes saw carpenters fitting wooden frames to prevent anyone from standing on the seat, but the authorities seem to have given up the unequal struggle on this point since then.

Yet the village bathhouse—something like the Finnish *sauna*—has been a flourishing institution for centuries, and through all the years when soap was scarce one had the impression that Russians were doing their best to keep clean in circumstances which would have made people from some countries give up entirely. On long train journeys everyone waits in an hour-long queue for the trickling tap, and if water gives out some of the men may dash out at the next stop to sluice themselves under a railway hose. One of the excuses offered for the large single-chamber lavatories is that it is easy to give them a thorough washdown, and that is in fact what they get.

At table one meets with old and new traditions, both pleasant and unpleasant, mingled together. Invitations to share a meal may be very courteous, with polite little Eastern bows, but you may find it hard to suffer the way your host eats his soup. Peasants may apologize engagingly for their clumsy, dirty hands yet when they share your table they may eat with a diffident delicacy, while next door an intellectual young man with a briefcase shovels up rice disgustingly with his knife. Indulgence in food and drink is comfortably regarded in most Russian circles. It is harder to get hold of drink than it used to be—and rightly so—but both police and public are still remarkably tolerant of drunken men. The average good citizen is represented in cartoons and advertisements as having a figure nearly as well-fed as Mr Khrushchev's, and if you make friends with Russians, whether men or women, they are certain some time to issue the old challenge: 'How many pancakes can you eat at a sitting?'

The break between old and new is clear and definite in another matter—the Soviet conventions about profanity. In 'polite society' —say, a good deal more than half of Soviet society in this context —one can resort to nothing worse than 'The Devil!' and 'Hell!' and 'Curse!' to relieve one's feelings. These words preserve some of their nineteenth-century strength in Russia, but to go further is simply taboo. When Eliza Doolittle is asked if she is walking across the park she replies, in the Russian translation, 'Chorta s dva!', which is approximately equivalent to 'Hell, no!' Monstrously unladylike, but not an expression snatched from over the borderline of the unspeakable, as Shaw intended. There is an impassable gulf between polite expletives and peasant or common expletives in Russian. Once you descend below such phrases as 'chorta s dva' all swearing is based on the ancient '. . . your mother' formula. Not that anyone's real mother need be involved. The peasant uses the expression if it starts to rain or if the sun is too hot, while for more serious occasions he can indulge in obscene and blasphemous elaborations of how he will wrong someone's mother. This is the immemorial kind of profanity; it probably lies at the bottom of the English taboo on the same word. Russian is not sophisticated enough to have developed, as the French have, some *mot de Cambronne* which is delicately balanced on the edge of shockability so that it is taboo enough to have a delicious force when needed, but not so taboo as to be unusable in ordinary circles. So at present it is not possible to render the full flavour of Eliza's word in Russian. Rude stories circulate among Russians, but they have not reached anything like the significance of the exchange of stories among Western men; the dividing line between the shocking and the unshocking is too sharp. The Russians have a tag equivalent to ' "Hell!" said the duchess . . .' but the duchess does not say 'Hell!'; she says '. . . your mother!'

The old swearing is being cleaned up; there is a strong teetotal and anti-smoking movement among the young; there are only occasional and unorganized prostitutes, and only rumours of orgies sometimes in very high society; there is nothing approaching pornography in the theatre, the cinema, or in print—there are not even any frivolous magazines nor the sort of paperbacks which Russians call 'literature of the boulevard'. Isn't 'puritan' the obvious label for this society where people appear to restrain so many of their impulses for the sake of the community, and where small children are put into uniform and taught to bow to their elders? Isn't 'puritan' the label for the people as well as for their authoritarian government, or the label at least for the leading, energetic, hard-working section of the people, who clean things up, make them run on tramlines, suppress as it would seem a lot of natural instincts, and persuade other people to do the same?

The discipline, the cleaning, and tidying-up are certainly going to continue, and by the most favourable possible interpretation they will continue for so long that it is impossible to foretell what other problems may not arise in the process. Nevertheless, I think it is incorrect to describe the Russians as puritanical, in spite of all their reticences and restraints; they are certainly not puritanical in the sense which the word has historically had in the West.

Russians may be reticent, reserved, shy, or severe for a purpose, but it is quite exceptional for any of them to indulge in austerity for what is called 'its own sake'. It is quite exceptional for any of them to show the self-lacerating, guilt-ridden asceticism which turns people into grey eminences or Nazi leaders. The teetotal young seem to be enjoying something positive, not repressive, when they try to persuade you not to drink; the reason for not drinking is in order to be able to throw oneself into something else. Young Russians have somewhat more freedom nowadays to try out a variety of personalities and attitudes to life, but few of them apparently choose to turn themselves into smug little section leaders.

When Russians are lazy or idle they seem to feel no guilt. When they have been completely abandoned to a temporary passion they seem to feel little remorse afterwards. Few of them are obsessively clean or tidy in the puritan manner. Few of them will pull in their belts in order to save for a future more than a few months away. Most of them are spendthrift with their money; when the State offered the alternative of interest-bearing loans or lottery loans without interest 'everybody', according to my Russian friends, wanted the lottery loan. Russians are permissive in bringing up young children, and when they do discipline them they are not trying to create a sense of guilt; they are simply trying to restore the child to the communal values. In short, they trust and believe in the goodness of human nature more than puritan peoples do.

Russians have their own traditional mistrust of human nature when they think it diverges too much from common standards. But puritanism of the Western kind has had almost no soil in which to grow in Russia. If Russian feudalism had weakened earlier than it did, and if the Old Believers had then become the dominant element in the new middle class of traders, they might perhaps have developed their Old Believer austerity into a conservative puritanism which could have matched the progressive puritanism of the West. But there was no such opportunity. The moral influence remained that of the established Orthodox Church, and 'Orthodoxy educates the heart, not the will'.

After all the chaos and tyranny which they have endured many Russians feel thankful for the existence of strict or formal social standards; they have themselves contributed to these standards, and the standards help to provide a mould for the individual; by voluntarily accepting some of them he gives his new liberties a new point.

It is particularly important, I think, to be clear about the conception of Russian or Soviet 'puritanism' when one looks at the relations between the sexes in Soviet Russia. It may seem natural to call this society puritanical where women do not flaunt, where nudity never appears, and delicacy of relations between the sexes seems often to be missing, but I must insist, for the reasons just given, that the word does not fit. The Englishman who said 'Not puritan but shy' was a great deal nearer the mark.

There have been self-torturing individuals and sects at times—even a castrating sect—in the Russian Church, but the Church in general has never been so much concerned with sin as many other Churches have; purity of heart has been more the theme. Priests are allowed to marry—'to marry one wife' is the canon—and on the whole sexual matters seem to have been left in a sort of elementary simplicity. (We are told, for instance, that it was common for couples to draw a little curtain in front of the ikon when they intended intercourse.)

A kind of innocence, secured by communal good nature, is still the dominant note. Even the crude young men, so blunt in their approaches, seem fundamentally innocent.

Innocent, it seemed to me, was the attitude to nudity when I first visited Russia in 1934. Bathing costumes were at that time almost unobtainable, but this did not prevent Russians from bathing in rivers and lakes as they have done for centuries. At an improvised bathing beach in the Moscow River men and women kept in groups ten or twenty yards apart, by tacit agreement, and bathed naked. (I was soon laughed out of wearing my own costume.) The girls were shy and tried to hide what they could as they went to the water, while the men peeped of course, and yet they were really shy too.

Such a scene may still be usual in the distant north or in parts of Siberia in summer, but it is no longer to be seen in centres which the foreigner is likely to visit. Bathing costumes became plentiful, and the natural reaction was that they are the proper dress for swimming and civilized people are expected to wear them. During the war bathing costumes were once more hard to get, but the clock was not turned right back for behaviour; on the Volga beach opposite Kuibyshev well-bred Soviet girls would swim in their petticoat, afterwards slipping a dry frock over it and going home by the ferry, cold and dripping underneath.

Most Russians, especially educated Russians, are by Western standards remarkably embarrassed about sex, nudity, or the private parts, but their embarrassment seems a natural modesty, not a repudiation due to self-discipline. When some of us became blood donors at Kuibyshev the doctor—a middle-aged man—put us through an exhaustive physical examination and asked questions about every ordinary disease; he must have examined at least several hundred donors on these lines, but when he came to ask if we had ever suffered from piles he blushed and stammered like any probationer nurse.

Sex instruction is a subject which both parents and authority seem to shy away from. There is no mention of it in several of the official textbooks for the training of teachers, nor in the Leningrad handbook for parents already quoted. At the Annual Congress of the International Scientific Film Association in Moscow in 1958 a Dutch scientific film on sex education was flatly refused projection. However, the famous educationist Makarenko had something to say about sex education in his lectures to parents. He suggests parents need not fear if their children get sex knowledge from other children and keep it secret; 'In this case secrecy is not to be feared!' At a suitable age fathers should talk to sons and mothers to daughters, but explanations which are too 'rational' should be avoided. 'Sexual love is based on other kinds of natural love—the true follows the true.' One may regard all this as elementary, innocent, or even mistaken but I do not think it can be called puritan.

Chasing women is not a national sport with Russians, though men from Soviet Georgia and Armenia have rather a name for it. Russia does not have the highly-developed lines of attack and defence which characterize relations between men and women in, say, Italy. Men and women can approach each other freely; 'anyone can speak to anyone in the Soviet Union', as one of my friends used to say, and yet there are conventions which regulate the approach. The Russian boy tilts his cap and grins in an obvious, good-natured way when he tries to make a pass at a girl, but unless he is drunk or a very hard case he will accept the girl's hand-off if she doesn't want to encourage him. Convention makes it easy for him to speak to her, but it also makes it easier for her to disengage, and easier for him to avoid feeling embarrassed if she does so.

Apart from a few gold-diggers and sophisticates Russian girls are usually modest in behaviour, attracting by a promised sweetness rather than by flaunting external charms. (The Nazis, among their loathsome statistics, claimed to have examined all the unmarried women when they captured the cities of Rostov and Novorossiisk, and to have established that 85 per cent of them were virgins.) Yet this modesty permits an approach which can sometimes knock a mere foreigner head over heels. Convention allows any of these modest girls to speak to a man first, to make the first approach—roguish or interested or casual—without any implication that she is a bad character. It would be quite improper, of course, for the man to respond by trying to raise the temperature at once; acquaintance proceeds experimentally, allowing either party openings for retreat, just as it does between Russians of the same sex.

One rather surprising method is practised sometimes outside theatres. It is so usual for theatres to be sold out in Russia that a brisk trade in returned tickets, or tickets alleged to be returned, is done outside the doors. An adventurous girl will sometimes buy two tickets for a popular play and offer to sell the second one to a latecomer whom she likes the look of. It is so common to buy tickets in this way that the man need have no suspicion that he is being picked up, and if the girl changes her mind by the time the lights go up on the first interval he need never know. Foreigners should be warned, however, that if when they are sitting at the end of a row in a theatre, an attractive girl seats herself on the gangway seat next to them just as the curtain goes up, she is not in the least inviting acquaintance. She is an actress, and by custom *strapontins* left unoccupied at the start of a performance may be taken by actors or actresses who want to see the play. If your Russian is good enough you may try conversational openings on her in the interval as you might with any other Russian, but attractive though the actress may be she will not much accord with a foreigner's idea of the profession; she will be more like, perhaps, the belle of an English girls' school with the bloom of her prefecthood still upon her.

Within the freedom which Russian convention allows it is not so necessary for a girl to flaunt, and delicacy between men and women can be a great deal more than one might imagine from a first sight of the rough sex equality so typical of Soviet life. Equality between the sexes is Soviet policy, of course, and in respect of equality before the law, equality in access to jobs, and so on, it is new. But there was a strong tradition of equality also before the Revolution—in the honourable, carefully fostered equality between the men and women of the old intelligentsia, and in the rough functional equality among peasants and industrial workers.

Peasant society was patriarchal, women could be roughly treated by their husbands, they took no part in government by the village Mir, and yet there was an equality in the hard life they all shared, in the necessary part played by women as well as men in the fields, and in the simple feeling that all belonged to the one community. One hears strikingly few jokes against women as women in Russia, in spite of the robust Russian sense of humour. There are jokes against the virago, the good-time girl, the lazy wife, the dress maniac, and other individual types, but very few against women in general, whether as a sex or as wives, mothers-in-law, colleagues, or drivers of cars. In principle every kind of job and every rank of job is open to women today, and this not uncommonly means that men find themselves working under a woman; to a foreigner it is remarkable how little this seems to be resented by Russian men, and what straightforward giving of orders and answering back there can be in these cases. Most wives, of course, go out to work as well as their husbands, so that the Western contrast between the mistress of the house and the master at work does not often arise.

In short, Russia is not a country of the sex war. Seventy per cent of Soviet doctors are women, men seem on the whole unjealous of women's position or status, and women behave as equals in conversation, arguing or asserting with a forthrightness which may seem to us unfemale but is merely Russian. All this equality is the background, one should remember, to the inferior status which so many women apparently have to accept in their work. Unskilled work in the Soviet Union seems most often to be done by women—the untrained or the unenterprising, perhaps —and few people seem to think it unfair that women should work at such jobs as spreading asphalt, portering luggage, sweeping the streets, or cleaning engines. Yet there is a kind of equal status in these simple women—they talk to you as people with their own independence and not as inferiors.

The community is the background for all, for women of education and refinement as well as the women who clear away the snow, and it is against this background that Russian women show themselves so often more womanly than English convention allows, though they may be less 'feminine' in the Western sense, less concerned about appearance and arts and wiles. One may see this even in some of the smartest and most sophisticated women in the country—the Intourist girls who deal with foreigners in the hotels. Their clothes and shoes are good, even their make-up and hairdressing are sometimes of good Western standard, they know they have a good appearance, they work very hard, and they have plenty of practice at stonewalling difficult foreigners. But when one of these rather frozen-looking young women takes a warmer interest in your request—probably because you have spoken to her in a Russian way—and she breaks into a sympathetic smile, she shows something simpler, more womanly and natural than the equivalent woman in England would show. The Englishwoman could be equally obliging, pleasant, good-hearted, but to exhibit these qualities so frankly, to unveil her essential female goodness to you in a sweetness like that of an Austrian or an Irish maid—that is not the English convention. If an Englishwoman felt she had so much sweetness showing she would probably be embarrassed, but a Russian woman is not embarrassed, because she is simply acting out of the sincerity which Russians show to each other as well as to foreigners.

The contrast is pointed, I think, by a minority of Intourist girls who become spoiled by the conditions of their work and who, abandoning some of their native standards, become harder, more egoistic, or more vulgar than their English opposite numbers usually are. These and similar girls in privileged jobs are the ones who can give short-term visitors the impression that 'Russian women are just as mad about clothes and just as exhibitionist as other women once they get the opportunity'. But it is a mistake to imagine that most young Russian women have been unconcerned about their appearance since the Revolution. It is a natural enough mistake in view of the generally drab and monotonous exterior which Russians of both sexes have presented and mostly still present. But the drabness and monotony are a generalized picture only. Care for personal appearance and interest in the spreading of fashions were rudimentary because there was so little to buy and so little time to spare, yet they were in essence the same sort of care and interest as in Western countries. It was only a minority of young women who scoffed, and even these severe, devoted types did not take to masculine attire. Within the general monotony one could find, for example, the spreading of a little fashion for a tiny Mary Queen of Scots collar to set off an ordinary black dress; at one time there would be a fashion for hair braided round the head, at another for an attempted revival of the nineteenth-century 'Greek' style; in one winter girls would all frame their faces in scarves tied over their fur caps, and in another they would ram the cap down on their heads and let their hair flow free from underneath. Simple though these fashions were, they were truly fashions, as a young Russian woman insisted to me once; and they circulated, as she said, without the help of women's magazines: 'Masha copied Sasha, and Natasha copied Masha, and then Galya and Irina and Olga copied Natasha. . . .' Western fashions filtered into Russia too, in spite of prohibitions; they filtered several years late, and diminished usually to simple general tendencies, but still to Russian women they represented something sharply new.

A whole essay could be made of the history of dress and attitudes to dress since the Revolution; it would incidentally provide one more kind of evidence, along with literature and music and all the arts, to show how Russians have always felt, even during the periods most hostile to foreign influences, to be still Europeans, still culturally part of Europe.

Now that Russian women are becoming able to dress better and with more individuality I think foreigners will become more aware of something which is fundamental to them, except for the exhibitionist minority. Apart from this minority it has always seemed to me that Russian women—even many Russian women outside the USSR—are unable and unwilling to bring themselves to that pitch of self-importance which comes so naturally to a Frenchwoman, for instance, and which the peak of Western fashionableness demands. (The same is true, of course, of Russian men.) Studied charm or dignity in Russian women seems nearly always to be relieved by some comfortable carelessness, some easy slurring over of final elegance, so that it is clear to you that they are presenting themselves not as 'appearance' but as something human, as women who for all their smartness are still part of the warm community. Only on certain formal occasions, when she is standing not for herself but for her nation or her group, a Russian woman may appear, by contrast, with a completely formal, rather stiff and cold exterior.

I think this attitude to personal appearance is likely to continue until there is a change in the bases of Russian society, and I also think the well-known reticences and shyness will remain in essence, even though Soviet Russians may be able to lead easier lives and to show relatively more variety of personality, more sophistication and self-possession than in the past. In more relaxed conditions it should be easier, indeed, for foreigners to convince themselves how the reticences and the shyness are neither basically puritan nor enforced from above. A comparison over the past thirty years may perhaps serve as illustration:

One of the truest films ever made about Russian life was Dovzhenko's *Earth*, in 1929. Many people in the West will remember its long poetic passages of southern countryside rich with apple harvest, and then at night the great moon dappling the shadows which fell on young peasant couples who stood in sandy corners, clumsy and silent, overcome with what welled within them, looking away from each other while standing clumsily close, neither daring to lay a finger on the other. This was a society perhaps just comprehensible to a Westerner but far removed from his experience, far removed in history, so to speak. Thirty years later, films such as *Teenagers* show an advance to what might be called a pre-1914 atmosphere; girls who might well be the daughters of some of those peasant couples are shown on the stairs of a Moscow tenement, exchanging embraces of deep love—for a few seconds, and probably only once in each film—with their young men. The first film kiss in 1956, and the first nude in a Soviet art exhibition at about the same time, were a sensation, according to foreigners who saw their reception by the public. The censorship which permitted these had relaxed indeed, but the young people themselves had been growing up too. They have in fact created their own problems which are partly the reason why such films as *Teenagers* are made. They are shy when one sees them nowadays daring sometimes to exchange loving gestures in public. They are shy although they have grown more sophisticated, but they are certainly not puritans. And their fathers and mothers in *Earth*, if one yields to the poetry of the film, were not puritans either, nor were you meant to see them as such.

The Russian sense of humour is more catholic than that of many peoples, sharper and finer than the Teutonic, less biting than the French, very close to the English in both its attitudes and its scope. It includes all kinds—irony, ridicule, fantastic exaggerations, 'blue' stories, jokes about professions or races or drunks, and of course such political themes as the laziness, corruptibility, or stupidity of officials. Ridicule is sometimes louder than it would be in England, but malice is strikingly absent. The stock comedian in Russia is either a poker-faced clown or a Ukrainian brimming over with Southern gusto and warmth.

In circulation there are classic stories known outside Russia, such as the one about the Chinaman, Russian, Englishman, German, and Jew who found flies in their soup; or native inventions such as the story of the two extremely drunken men who became friends over vodka, were delighted to find that they were both called Ivan Ivanovitch Ivanov, quarrelled violently when each of them alleged that he lived at No. 39 Bashkirskaya Street, and finally drank themselves into the realization that they were father and son. The 'dumb sniper' was the hero of several war-time stories; he couldn't understand why there was a statue to Pushkin: 'He lost the duel, didn't he?' Another wartime theme was the good-time girl—'Of course I'm looking grand. I eat in the American style (*po amerikanski*); I get shoes in the Italian style (*po italianski*); I dress in the English style (*po angliiski*)—and I undress in commercial style (*po kommercheski*).

The broad humour tolerated on the Soviet stage would surprise those who regard Russia as a nation of grim-faced Molotovs and Gromykos. There are sometimes passages which would hardly pass the English censor, in contemporary comedies, or in Maya-kovsky's play *The Bug*. In the old favourite *Uncle's Dream* (dramatized from a story by Dostoievsky) the supposedly rich uncle waddles painfully on to the stage, complaining audibly about the affliction which my Kuibyshev doctor could not men-tion without a blush. Variety theatres are few, but they often put on an evening devoted entirely to revue-length sketches. In one such performance, among the usual gibes at lazy managers, American politicians, and parents who pull strings for their sons, there were several sketches as 'Western' as the following:

The scene is the waiting room of a maternity ward. Among the nervous fathers one Kalmanov is almost in a state of collapse. An astrologer had told his wife before she was married that if her first child was a girl all would be well for ever after, but if it was a boy the father would die. His wife had insisted on having her baby just the same, and Kalmanov is consoled by the other fathers and by an orderly who brings vodka. The double doors swing open at last and a beaming nurse announces: 'Citizen Kalmanov! It's a boy!' The orderly falls dead. Curtain.

I have made much of certain features of Russian manners and morals, partly because the visitor is more likely to come across these, but also because they help to show how, in a society with the strong communal loyalties of the Russians, people are likely to be addicted to a different pattern of human weaknesses and virtues from those in societies where individualism is more dominant. If some earnest missionary were to examine the Russian people for their proneness to the Seven Deadly Sins I think he would have to award them only very small black marks in respect of Pride, Envy, Avarice, and Lechery; a slightly blacker one for occasional Anger; a fair-sized one for Gluttony; and the only really bad one for a still very widespread Accidie—not so much in its old form of hopeless laziness and despair, but as a substratum still showing in all the indifference, the petty adherence to rule, the reluctance to find out the true nature of things, and the tendency to talking instead of doing, which are still characteristic of at least a large minority of Russians.

They are encouraged in these tendencies by the ramifications and multiplication of authorities under the Soviet system, and by the absence of representative institutions except at very low levels. If people want proper attention they have to depend upon correctly interpreting and exploiting the machine—a machine which can often function very badly—and they have to become experts in assessing the status and pliability of the various officials. If they are unjustly treated they can, and do, appeal to their trade union, their local newspaper, or their local representative in the Supreme Soviet, but the process of appeal can be a very long one. It is often easier to resort to the bribery, corruption, and knavery which are so widespread and which nowadays constitute the chief internal 'enemy' of the Soviet state.

Even when one is dealing with Russian officials, however, it is often possible to appeal to their human brotherliness and charity; if you offer passionate sincerity you may be met with understanding. In other kinds of personal relationship Russians retain all that refreshing spontaneity and straightforwardness of which I spoke earlier; since the political relaxation they are able to show it even more than they used. It has often been asked whether genuine friendship between individuals is possible in Russia, in face of so much state regulation and suspicion and the general sense of all belonging to the same crowd. But any Russian would raise his eyebrows in surprise at the question. What does one ask of friendship—a mirror, a critic, a complementary half, an audience, someone who needs you as you need him? In Russia you can have them all. There is not the same nervousness about the group as there appears to be in America, where the visitor can become depressed at feeling that so much warm but superficial 'friendliness' is not personal to him, but is due to a deep-seated convention which determines that every stranger must be treated in the same way lest a great American principle be violated. In Russia, in spite of all the group solidarity and egalitarianism, it is not assumed that every individual must be somehow in sympathy with every other. (Nor, if two men find themselves in particular sympathy with each other, are they liable to be suspected of homosexuality.)

There is a pleasant dignity about friendship with a Russian. You have made friends slowly and tentatively, you have not invaded each other's privacy in the possessive way so common for instance among Germans, you have been sincere but not sentimental, frank but not self-humiliating, you have not been exclusive, your Russian friend has introduced you into his group (but you have remained *his* friend)—when you separate you must separate, and after fourteen years you can go back and pick up a friendship almost exactly where you left off.

There can be danger in friendship, of course. One of the first questions asked by the security police is 'Who are your friends?' They ask this when they have arrested you, or when they are trying to recruit you, as a patriotic citizen, to do some spying for them. In the past people very often had to be careful about making friends until each knew how far the other was inclined to be 'political'. This mistrust was not simply because you felt that you might some day express criticism of the régime. If a man was going to betray you he might do so on no evidence at all, since 'political offenders' were often charged on evidence so flimsy that they could not possibly have foreseen their arrest.

Yet during the worst periods ties of friendship among Russians were impressive and powerful; I believe most Russians would at any time have put personal loyalties first if they could, and would have tried to protect their friends when it was at all possible. The comparative uselessness of the system in discovering real political offenders seems now to have been recognized, at least for the time being, and such devices as the domestic spy network—three persons unknown to each other in every house block—are thought at the time of writing to have disappeared as a general thing, though they have left an aftermath of apprehension among middle-aged and older persons.

The Russians, taking their community as part of the air they breathe, regard individual friendships as a matter of course; and they have no difficulty, either, in accepting individuals who are distinguished in talent, tastes, or sensibility as also members of the community. Whether such people are of proletarian or old upper-class stock matters little nowadays. Every time I have been in Russia I have tried to conduct a private poll on the extent to which, according to my limited powers of judgment, the social origins of people whom I met seemed to be discernible. My mistakes were almost always of the same kind; I think most Western visitors would find, as I did, that although one would almost never mistake a person of aristocratic or bourgeois origin for a person of peasant or worker origin, one would very often fall into the opposite error, wrongly deducing, from one's Western basis, that persons of such refinement or imagination would be unlikely to have come from a peasant or working-class family.

In the earlier days a host of natural talents and sensibilities were brought to light in such families and trained in a hurried way, with results which were often charming. Casual acquaintances in trains would shyly reveal 'I am a poet' and recite verses which they had composed, on some heroic theme, in a style well above that of the verse in an English provincial newspaper. The young man who had at last acquired a musicial instrument, in those days of shortage, was as one with the philosopher's stone in his hands—he, a homeless orphan, would open up the whole world of meaning in music and play in a Moscow orchestra too. A half-starved young man in a tunic made out of a tablecloth had read *David Copperfield* and *Hamlet*—how he admired English culture! I met a young peasant woman with a gift for languages who had been drafted at an early age into an office where she dealt with foreigners; she had just discovered the word *nuance* and lingered over it affectionately, sadly remarking that the conception of a nuance did not seem to exist in the minds of foreigners whom she met from certain countries, though she recognized it in the everyday attitudes of Swedes, Englishmen, and Frenchmen.

Since those days the eager, gifted young have been put through solid training courses, lasting five years or more, if they wish to enter the artistic professions, while more than a generation of ordinary, ungifted young people have been exposed to some elementary education in literature, music, and the arts, on the principle that everyone is capable of some appreciation of these.

The limitations on experiment in the arts are so depressing in the Soviet Union, and so much has been made abroad of the restrictions on Pasternak, Dudintsev, Shostakovitch, and others, and of the moral and political purposes so often assigned to the arts in Soviet education, that it has often been overlooked what enormous work has been done inside the country in fostering interest and spreading opportunities for appreciation and practice of the arts, albeit on restricted lines, among the ordinary population. There never seem to be enough copies of any classical book to meet the demand, so large has the reading public become; an edition of 300,000 copies of a new translation of Shakespeare's sonnets disappears in a very short time, and people queue to put their names on the subscription lists which are opened, in advance of publication, for translations of the collected works of Thomas Mann, Anatole France, Stendhal, or Flaubert. Musical instruments are no longer worth their weight in gold, but the demand for them—largely for use in amateur music clubs—seems insatiable. On a lesser scale painters and sculptors find it easy to sell their works, unoriginal though so many of them are, and shops find it easy to sell classical reproductions to a public which does not easily come by any pictures at all, not even of the lowest merit, in the way that the Western public does through magazines and advertising literature that goes into the dustbin. But the greatest Russian interest—after reading, and after sport and dancing for the young—goes into the theatre. The country is covered with amateur dramatic clubs, whose talents seem to arise less from exhibitionism, than from what might be called the national passion for human nature. The differentiation between the amateur and professional stage is less marked in Russia than in Britain or many other countries; both amateurs and professionals seem inspired by a similar enthusiasm for all sorts of characters and for perfecting their presentation of them.

The official 'line' on the arts has of course relaxed somewhat during the years since Stalin's death. A directive to 'discover the best light foreign literature' has resulted in the translation into Russian of *The Quiet American, Our Man in Havana, Lucky Jim, Look Back in Anger*, and *Hurry On Down*. The best of the rich collection of Impressionist paintings are on show again in Moscow, and the explanatory notes on the wall no longer speak of the styles of Matisse and Van Gogh as 'reflecting the increasing degeneracy of the bourgeois world', as used to be the case. The Impressionists, in the new version, 'followed more and more new paths, often subjective in character', they 'turned away from social problems', but their revolt against academic routine is described as 'very important'. Marquet is praised for his 'lyrical rendering of landscape', while the 'exceptionally complicated and contradictory' Picasso is praised for the 'deep feeling for humanity' in his earlier works, though they were followed by the 'formal tendencies' of his cubism.

There is an official reaction also—in the press and in educational works—against the vulgar paper flowers, crude statuettes, 'sugary picture postcards', or 'pictures of unnatural swans against a poisonously-bright landscape' which are so often offered to the Soviet consumer. 'Why do women not realize,' says the magazine *Ogonyok*, 'that their most tasteful ensembles are "killed" by these crudely flowering wallpapers in colours of poached egg and spring onion?' There is a rich soil for the appreciation of the arts, and a fascinating book could be made if some well-equipped foreigner were permitted to spend a couple of years in Russia, travelling everywhere in complete freedom, talking to the public and to teachers as well as to people engaged in the arts, and reporting on people's enthusiasms, on the abstract sculptures and experimental poetry which are produced in private by a few, and on the occasional preference for clean, simple modern lines in theatre décor or shop design, as well as on the academic pictures, the vulgar china vases, the second-rate novels and dance tunes, and so on.

It is impossible to forecast how far the new relaxations may be allowed to develop in the arts, as in every other field. But even in a much freer situation than the present some fundamental tendencies in Russian taste would be likely to persist.

In the first place the wonderful flowering of literature, music, and the theatre in nineteenth-century Russia has often obscured for foreigners the small stature of the forerunners of that great century, and the delayed development of the whole gamut of the arts. But Russians are well aware of this. They have men still alive and lecturing who personally knew Tolstoy and Tchehov, Tchaikovsky and Rimsky-Korsakov; the whole great period is felt to be involved with the immediate roots of present-day Russia. In Britain if our taste turns for a time against the Victorians we can go back to Swift and Pope, or to the Metaphysical Poets; in Russia there were no poets contemporary with the Metaphysicals, and the contemporaries of Swift and Pope were such undistinguished writers that only scholars would read them now. In Britain it is the Tudor period which stands, in the popular mind, for the romance of the comfortably far-off past—half-timbered houses, Tudor halls, doublets and farthingales, Shakespeare and Good Queen Bess. But the same period in Russia, the period of Ivan the Terrible and Boris Godunov, was still part of the Middle Ages, and it feels as far off to modern Russians as our own Middle Ages do to us—perhaps farther, in fact, because Russia has preserved so few medieval churches or buildings compared with

England. Many famous Russian towns were founded only in the fourteenth century, and there simply are not enough old objects in Russia to provide the same continuous feeling of history as in Western countries. The earlier history is not missing altogether; it lives on in a feeling for the heroic Kievan period, for Peter the Great and Catherine, and in some colourful, barbaric survivals such as St Basil's Cathedral, but the history which you can still feel around you in many Russian cities, the history which gives the young a nostalgia for a romantic past, is no further back than the Romantic Period itself—the time of Pushkin, Lermontov, and the Decembrists, of the defeat of Napoleon and *War and Peace*, and the beautiful Palladian buildings which are preserved almost everywhere.

It is the period of Pushkin above all, because he is the greatest and also the most typically Russian writer—more finished, more convincing in his sympathies than Byron with whom the Russians always compare him, a sophisticated-simple figure with no English equivalent, the perfectly disciplined romantic, the Mozart of Literature. Pushkin is to the Russians what Shakespeare is to the English, and he is nearer to them in time and in language than Shakespeare is to us. Grandparents of people now living might have met Pushkin, and his verse can be so timeless that young girls, following Tatiana's lead in *Eugene Onegin*, today still copy out the first lines of her famous letter: 'I am writing to you; what else is there to say? . . . etc.' and send them to the young man on whom they first set their heart.

Pushkin in literature and Tchaikovsky in music above all others release the Russian soul. They have given a form and a voice to the untrained emotions of hundreds of thousands who must have felt much as Nicholas Ostrovsky did (the hero of the Civil War who wrote *How the Steel was Forged*):

You know why I love music?—I have seen a great deal of blood and suffering in my life. It was my fate to grow up in a hard time. We spared neither the enemy nor ourselves. . . . I have known very little love. And here comes Tchaikovsky and opens up in me such intimate feelings, awakens such tender thoughts whose very existence I never suspected.

This is a release which responds to the needs of simple people struggling into their own individualities, it echoes the Russian feeling for human comradeship, and it affects many of the artists —executants or creators—in contemporary Russia as well as their public. When the average Russian orchestra play Bach or Corelli they seem to be trying to impose some emotional phrasing of their own instead of submitting themselves entirely to the discipline of Bach or Corelli and letting the crisp outline delight the heart. When they play jazz they romanticize it too. On the stage the typical décor for the ordinary play tends to romance rather than realism. If it is a comedy of young love the birch trees shimmer in keeping; if it is Goldoni's *La Locandiera* the scene is brilliant with strongly sunlit walls and unnaturally large southern fruits and flowers; if it is a play about an old professor, untidiness and faded old-fashioned surroundings may be used to enhance his character in a Dickensian way.

The heroic is not found embarrassing. When, towards the end of the war, Russian troops were recapturing towns from the Germans almost every day, the news was given out by loud-speaker on each occasion, all over the cities. Patriotic music came first, and the actual announcement was splendidly pronounced, with rhetorical effects of the kind which a more sophisticated and sceptical nation, such as the English, will nowadays only find acceptable on the occasion of a coronation. In England we needed the astringent tones of a Churchill, with their hint of satire or irony, to rouse us or convince us that all was going well; the Russians could take their heroics neat.

A melancholy strain, equally, can be indulged in without embarrassment or always falling into sentimentality. Again during the war, when one was not supposed to mention in public the possibility of low morale or the need for 'comfort', the girls who worked in my office would gather round the lamp in the evenings and relieve their souls in a sad Ukrainian song:

And at the same period, with posters still urging young men in the bluntest terms to avenge the invasion, a magazine for young people reprinted the old song of the dying coachdriver:

On almost any evening at that time one could—and one can still—live out one's sorrows in the music of Tchaikovsky, either in a concert hall or at the opera or ballet. 'Greater than Beethoven', many Russians say of Tchaikovsky, and there seems not the slightest sign of any diminution in his popularity.

Russian taste is certain to be dominated, for a very long time at least, by a natural sympathy for the romantic approach, for the direct appeal to the feelings. Not that the quality of the appeal is always at the level of Tchaikovsky or Pushkin, nor is its debasement due always to political interference. I have often thought the work of the average portrait photographer one of the truest indices of popular taste in any country, and in Russia the photographer's windows—unaffected, one would presume, by political directives—still offer poses of bogus heroism, expressions of facile sentimentality, and 'romantic' backgrounds which all seem to have changed very little since before the First World War. A great deal of Soviet popular music, fiction, and painting, whether 'political' or not, has a similar unrefined sentimental quality, and it appeals to a large, undiscriminating public. The cultural patterns are still being groped for, since so much of the peasant culture has disappeared and there has not been much time to spare, as yet, for the development towards a self-confident urban or industrial culture with something, say, of the sardonic humour and cheekiness of the Cockney or the Berliner. One of the most popular plays on the Russian stage is a dramatization of *Pickwick Papers*; it is well done with one significant exception—the only character not properly presented is Sam Weller, who is made into a Figaro of a more aristocratic period. The Cockney flavour has not been understood.

There are city jokes, of course, about bus-conductresses and football matches and foremen, there is some city cynicism, and in caricatures and stories one sometimes sees the germ of a conception of the 'little man', but it is too soon yet to see what kind of an urban-industrial culture may eventually shape itself out of universal education and the strains and pressures of city life, out of old solidarities and the new acquiring of personal possessions.

The traditions of peasant culture have weakened a great deal—much more than the traditions of peasant morality or peasant society. (It was a limited culture anyway, and the whole development of the arts in Russia suffered badly because of the limitations of popular culture, and the class barrier to the extension of any other kind.) Folk-song provided a harvest of themes for composers from Glinka onwards, but nowadays the music of these composers is more likely to be preferred to the folk-songs. When in 1945 I saw a team of Russian folk-singers, in old-fashioned smocks, performing before an audience of young people in Moscow, they had a warm reception but the songs seemed to be felt as somewhat 'quaint'; they were already some way towards the artificial position which folk-songs and Morris dancing occupy in England. The folk-song strain has been developed in our own day by Alexandrov, founder of the Red Army choir, and by some other composers, in dozens of songs of a 'national' flavour of which some, such as *Steppe Cavalry*, have become well known abroad. People in Russia like these tunes, but as the music director of Moscow Radio once pointed out to me, they don't whistle them much nor sing them in the street. What the average person prefers are less rousing, more comfortable tunes such as the well-established 'Kto yevo znaet?' ('Who Knows Who It Was?')

As to the decorative arts, the new personal possessions demonstrate what a transitional stage has been reached. The themes of peasant decoration can still flourish pleasantly in the design of fabrics, china, and *objets d'art*, but they are outnumbered by themes debased from old bourgeois taste, along with themes from the Asiatic republics of the Soviet Union, a few new themes filtering through from East Germany, Finland, Czechoslovakia, and Hungary, and a lot of sheer vulgar invention on the themes of the tractor, the banner, the physical culture parade, and so forth. What people are after, probably, is colour, and some recognizable representational shapes in their homes which have been so long empty of all but essentials. The overblown vases, spotted pink pigs, ancient warriors, Cossack horsemen, swans and simpering children and gilded busts of Marx and Lenin are easily classed by a foreigner as 'Victorian'; what is impossible is to extract from them any characteristics which could fairly be taken to typify 'contemporary Russian design'. The 'Victorian' label fortunately does not apply to all; there are a few simple, well-shaped cups and saucers as well as overdecorated ones; some kitchen utensils and appliances where, perhaps, no one has thought about decoration, achieve a good functional appearance; some matchbox designs, among the hundreds which now make Russia a philumenist's paradise, have a charming simplicity suited to their size; and there are one or two newly furnished places—a record shop and a café in the Nevsky Prospekt, and in Moscow a bookshop, an art gallery, and some of the demonstration flats at the Building Exhibition—in cool modern idioms of steel and glass and canvas and wood. What is going to be typically Russian, however, no one can say; the artists and dress designers and their most discriminating customers seem to have no more idea than the general public, except that they all continue to praise the best products of peasant handicraft.

The whole of the Russian art and literary world, both producers and public, is at present simmering with discussion, and it is open, sensitively if a little nervously open, to foreign influences as never before since the Revolution. Artists and writers still produce didactic works, but they have no need to feel so self-consciously didactic as they used, since education has by now given them such a wide, demanding, and discussing public, and the political leadership does not, at least for the present, insist on such direct expression of ideological content. The difference is that plays, novels, films, and paintings are far more concerned with the problems of individual human beings than they used to be. They may still be 'ideological' but they mostly express the ideology through the situations of human individuals rather than through organizational symbols and problems. This preoccupation with individual moral situations is partly dictated by the present Party line, but it has naturally opened the doors to a flood of more humane novels, plays, and works of art—good and bad— which it would be extremely difficult for the authorities to check if they ever wanted to. It is not surprising that there is so much uneasiness about the limits which are to be allowed, yet the significant thing even about Dudintsev's *Not By Bread Alone*, it seemed to me, was his concern for the individual rather than the fact that he attacked the bureaucracy and got in trouble for it.

The curiosity about foreign works seems to know no bounds. Abstract artists or tachistes from Poland are usually found laughable, but some Russian artists at least want to see their work in case they might themselves miss some spark which could kindle a response. Ignorance lends a good deal of enchantment, and the name of James Joyce seems to be a sort of talisman for many who can know almost nothing of his work. A few pages of *Ulysses* were translated in one of the literary reviews during the 1930's, and to my knowledge one copy of *Ulysses* in English and one of *Portrait of the Artist* were circulating at the same time, though these are very likely to have been destroyed during the purges. Yet now Kolotozov, director of *The Cranes Are Flying*, alleges that in that film he was trying 'to do something of what Joyce did with words'. It is difficult for a foreigner to know what this can mean, especially if he compares Kolotozov's work with that of Cocteau or the early Buñuel for instance. By our standards it is a fairly ordinary, moving film. It does make a poetic use of images from time to time—suggestively in a simple way, instead of directly as in the usual Russian film, and this difference, an obvious one to Russians though small, must be what caused Kolotozov to make his extraordinary comment.

Russians of any culture—and some of almost none—are very conscious of the extent to which they have been out of touch with Western development in the arts since the Revolution. Even those who still indulge in nationalistic boasting are often well aware of this. It is a situation which imposes a delightful but serious responsibility on anyone who comes into contact with Russians, and a responsibility which it may fall to the most innocent tourist to share. Russians are in such an omnivorously receptive state at the moment that it seems extremely important that when we meet them we should bear in mind what an innocent earnestness they bring to the arts. They are bred on Tolstoy, Tchehov, and Turgenev, whom they read in their teens; if they are at all interested in criticism they have the example of more than a century, from the all-powerful Belinsky onwards, in holding as an act of faith that the primary duty of the arts is to reform people and institutions. On the other hand most of them are so little educated in the forms of art that they indiscriminately accept almost any manifestation of the arts in the past. They are not much inclined to put one style against another. They are not put off, for example, by the Art Nouveau buildings in the old bourgeois quarters, whose carefully preserved stucco still spawns bulbous flowers and submarine macaroni.

So when they come to the arts of the contemporary West they may well want to be shown everything which is going on. They certainly want to see how amusing or lighthearted we can be. But I think it is something of a duty to bring especially to their notice our writers and artists who speak to the heart, who show some compassionate sympathy for human nature and some belief in its capacity for good—Forster, Lawrence, Cary, Arthur Miller, Mauriac, Chamson, perhaps Camus, in literature, and in painting some of the neo-romanticists, for instance, or the leading Australians. Too much acquaintance with our amoral dissections or with our concentration on the subjective in the plastic arts could lead to a serious revulsion from the West. Russians are not well acquainted with what preceded these tendencies, and not many of them would be willing to accept them as temporary and technical explorations.

The Soviet authorities for reasons of their own might take the opportunity of formulating the revulsion and turning it into a prohibition, but it would have a genuine foundation in the taste of the public, much as they might regret the ringing down of another curtain on the West. It is significant that, while 'formalistic' experiments of Western artists are nowadays sometimes mentionable in magazines, and in the Hermitage one can see early cubist paintings by Picasso, similar experiments by Russian artists in the free years after the Revolution are not to be seen in public nor reproduced in art magazines. Knowledge of these Russian experiments circulates privately, but if the curtain were to come down again it would thus be foreign and not Russian artists who could be condemned in public.

After such a revulsion the Russian arts might sink into sentimentality again; or if a genius or two appeared we might see a Tolstoy or a Courbet of our day. Even if there is to be no great revulsion I think, since the Russians have skipped so much in the last forty years, and since they have in that time made so much of their new society, they are unlikely to want to go through the stages they have missed, even if a few Russian artists were to become enthusiasts for Post-Impressionism, Cubism, abstract art, and so forth. I see no likelihood of another Kandinsky or Malevitch arising in Russia, even in private isolation, for much the same reasons that there will not be another Kandinsky or Malevitch in the West. Nor will there be a return to the time when machines, because they were new, were for a brief period the themes of works of art—the cream-separator in one section of *The General Line*, or a whole factory in Mossolov's *Music of the Machines*.

The accent will continue to be on the human, for reasons which I have laboured often enough in this book. And the human, almost certainly, will be explored more delicately, more intimately, and above all more as a matter of individual personality than in the past. In 1960 more than half the contemporary plays on the Soviet stage had a boy-meets-girl theme or a triangle theme. (Three of them dealt with middle-aged husbands attracted by young girls, each play offering a different solution.)

There has always been a strong preference in Russia, but especially during the Soviet period, for paintings of subjects involving human *situations*—the Zaporozhe Cossacks of Repin, the pyramid of skulls and other anti-war pictures by Verestchagin, and the long-drawn agony of The Ninth Wave by Aivazovsky, as well as all the later paintings of gleaming Soviet achievements (though these are now sometimes caricatured in *Krokodil*). But the Impressionists now hang in some of the most prominent places in the galleries of Moscow and Leningrad, and I think their freshness is likely to bring a reaction against the overemphasis on subjects of human situation, just as it brought a reaction, on the first appearance of the Impressionists in Europe, against the prevalence of the pathetic fallacy in Salons and Academies. For what, in fact, could be more human, more inspired by the delicacy of a human touch than, say, Renoir's rendering of some overlooked hedge-corner? Until now the usual Soviet attitude to such a painting was that it was the work of a soul maiming itself in contemplation away from the world of men. But now that Russians can relax a little, now that they do not need the security of the mass quite as much as they used, now that they can look at each other more as individuals, I think the Impressionist painter is likely to be valued for his rare and precious eye serving as a telescope to hitherto unobserved delights. Pictures of 'human situations' will not become entirely out of date, but I think the conception of the human will be enlarged in this way and will inspire Soviet artists, as it has indeed inspired a few in the past. There is a similar discovery of the poetry and even the uniqueness of individual experience in recent films and novels; it has been there all the time in the work of a very few unfashionables such as Pasternak. It is a discovery which the Russians, with all their long-established sincerity, are just about ripe to make and to exploit in all the arts. In due course it may bring about another reaction towards the mass and towards art based on 'Human situations', but the advance which one may hope to see made in the near future is not likely to be entirely lost.

8

Russians and Their Government

IT IS A rare occasion for most Russians when they meet a foreigner, and among the mass of questions which they ask there are often some rather blunt political ones such as 'Why does your country oppress Negroes?', 'Why won't your country accept our disarmament proposals?' and so forth. Other Russians, when they have made friends with a foreigner, will bring up political matters from the opposite point of view and unburden themselves, though usually with some reserve, about injustices committed by their Government. A third political approach which the visitor is bound to meet is that of the Intourist guide, who is in duty bound to make discreet propaganda for the Soviet system, so that the three kinds of approach can together convey the impression that Russians must spend a lot of their time talking about capitalism, communism, foreign imperialism, and so on.

Such general themes, however, are not in the least typical of ordinary Russian conversation. In the early days of the Revolution the country naturally seethed with political discussion, and some discussion of policy, so long as it was Communist policy, went on well into the time of the First Five-Year Plan. But the purges of 1935-8 put an end to all that. The discussion of policy as a matter of pro and con became too dangerous, and the Party rules forbid it even in Party branch meetings. Since only a handful of Soviet citizens play any part in deciding policy there seems no reason why discussion of this kind should revive unless in the greatest privacy. The 'line' is laid down through the press, radio, schools, and public lectures, and it is so universally publicized that when people read the newspaper it is significant that they very often turn to the foreign news page first; they know only too well what the rest of the paper will contain.

Yet though Russians have to accept policy, and political discussion in the Western sense is almost excluded, they are far from being passive in their attitudes to their Government and its policies. Their first reaction to any new policy is—'What is behind it? What is safe for us to do?' These, it is reported, were the questions people asked each other when Stalin died; they were also the questions asked when one of the nineteenth-century Tsars died. Russians have become adept at reading between the lines of communiqués, and they can estimate impending policy changes by noticing the dropping of a slogan or the non-appearance of a familiar Kremlin figure at an important gathering.

When Russians attend meetings they are not as emotionally exploitable as one might expect. They show enthusiasm for processions, they cheer in the right places but not too much, and they never give that impression which one used to get from Fascist crowds—of atoms ready to be burned up into one great molecule. When they feel it is safe to do so Russians rise spontaneously to a noble occasion, of victory or celebration; on VE-Day they broke into the courtyard of the British Embassy and demanded a speech from some representative of their ally. But demonstrations and cheering have never been much encouraged by the Soviet authorities, probably because they could soon become double-edged, and since the early days the leaders have rarely indulged in crowd oratory. In the summer of 1944 a column of 55,000 German prisoners was marched through the streets of Moscow to give the people some taste of victory, but they were asked to refrain from any loud demonstrations. Personally I thought the procession one of the most dramatic things I have ever witnessed, but the people of Moscow remained mostly quiet, though a few of them called out homely insults and a few others uttered gasps of surprise. Yet the crowd seemed neither sullen nor repressed.

As I said earlier, Russians are not usually people who like accepting discipline more than is absolutely necessary. They have always been quick to take advantage of loopholes and quick to sense which officials or which orders need not be taken too seriously. Even a foreigner will come across instances. He is sure to overhear some of the long arguments about queues and exits and entrances; in a café he may notice the public turning a completely deaf ear to the 'agitator' at the bar who is making a speech to recruit volunteers for military training; or he may witness such incidents as the 'home guard' drilling of Bolshoi Theatre dancers which I saw in wartime in the public square at Kuibyshev, where the ballerinas, giggling and fooling, made the young officer blush and turned the whole thing into a farce.

As for discipline which cannot be so openly flouted, it is well known what ingenuity the Russians have shown in what they call *kombinatsia*—arrangements arrived at by persuasion of the right persons, with or without a bribe. When the 'norms' were too high for the average worker to achieve, a good-natured foreman would discover 'conditions of special difficulty' demanding a lower norm, or a book-keeper might manipulate the returns. When Siberian camp life became unbearable for some of the weaker inmates the camp doctor would slip them into hospital for a rest, just as camp doctors did when Dostoievsky was a prisoner. Responsibilities could be—and no doubt still often are— shunted on to so many lines of the organizational network that discrepancies and defalcations might never be brought home to any particular person. The whole system of under-the-counter deals, illegal exchanges, and oiling of palms is known collectively as *blat*, and *blat* flourished, of course, long before the Revolution. In Soviet times we know of it not only from the reports of re-fugees but from the thousands of instances which are exposed in the Soviet press and radio as examples for punishment, and from Soviet plays and films which are devoted to the exposing of these abuses, implying at the same time that there must be a great deal to expose. It has not always been noticed abroad how bad administration, apathy, straightforward individualism, and *blat* have together slowed down many Soviet campaigns for industrial or agricultural progress and caused some of them to be abandoned. Some campaigns have had to be repeated, though in a version made to look new, and more than two versions have had to be tried in the attempt (for the present abandoned) to make peasants give less attention to their private plots, or the attempt to get senior schoolchildren somehow linked with industry in a practical way.

And all this has gone on while the Soviet nation as a whole—including all the people involved in *blat*—has built up a production of pig-iron 10 times, of oil 12 times, of coal 16 times, and of electric power 123 times the pre-revolutionary figures, besides defeating the Germans, making good most of the damage they inflicted, and maintaining peacetime armaments on a huge scale. The whole stupendous achievement is a tribute partly to dictatorship, partly to genuine enthusiasm among a large minority, partly to education, but partly also to an extraordinary fact about the Russian people—extraordinary, that is, to most people from the West, though it does not strike Russians as extraordinary. It is this—that in spite of all the oppression, individual suffering, and shortages, in spite of all the shifts people have been put to to satisfy their simplest needs, basically they have nearly all of them retained the sense of belonging to one great Russian community, and they have in a rough way identified their community with the State. Many of the people who have suffered most, and most unjustifiably, at the hands of the Soviet system, have distinguished themselves later by their patriotism and self-sacrifice for the nation, as though they were obliged to convince themselves that Russia, after all, was in the right. An intellectual who spent six years in a labour camp for an almost unidentifiable 'political offence' told me: 'The thing on which I concentrated most when I was away was to convince myself that my incarceration was not the fault of our Government, but only of certain individuals.'

This remarkable loyalty to the common cause is not incompatible with *blat*, because *blat* seems to arise mostly from the pressure of situations rather than from officials who are abusing their position in order to enrich themselves (though there is naturally a minority who try to do just this). There are so many good turns done partly for a consideration and partly just as good turns; there are so many good turns done to individuals, in perversion of the rules, for no consideration at all. Even ex-prisoners tell of the risks sometimes taken by security officials in order to give relief to a prisoner who could offer nothing in return.

The blend of mass loyalty and *blat* shows how far most Russians are from wanting or even understanding a system of representative government of Western form. To a limited extent they do choose their own representatives, but they choose them as men and women and not as supporters of policies. They choose their representatives at the lowest levels in trade union and Party branches and local Soviets, and though so far as one can hear they very rarely choose them by a vote between two or more candidates, their choice is in fact sifted through communal feeling until it reaches the point where one nomination seems obvious, in the same way that things were done in the Mir. Russians account this system a choice, and when the candidate is eventually nominated it is always possible to vote against him. The Government attaches great importance to this 'selection of representatives from below', and the press sometimes reports cases of new elections being ordered where the nominated candidate was found to have been imposed by a higher authority and not 'chosen from below'. Soviet citizens also vote in larger units for their representatives in the Supreme Soviet, the Soviet of their Republic, and so forth, but here they have much less chance of acquaintance with persons who might win the nomination.

In Berlin in 1945, when the Four-Power authority was organizing a free trade union set-up for the city, the British representative proposed that there should be elections, but the Russian representative objected that if seven people are nominated and there are only six seats, then the people who want the seventh man 'will not be represented'. The Russian's use of this argument was probably not altogether ingenuous, since it was his job to get candidates of the right political colour elected if possible, but his choice of such an argument to convince a British officer most clearly demonstrates the gulf between their points of view. The sophisticated idea of the seesaw between parties seems beyond the grasp of all but a few Russians, probably because they have no experience in their own history of a change of government other than by force. Most of them seem to think of political parties—if they think about them at all—as bodies determined to achieve power by fair means or foul, or else as the tools of some other power seekers. In either case it seems to them irresponsible to put the government of one's country at the mercy of a popular choice between such factions. It was a Tass correspondent long established in London, and familiar with parliamentary debates, who expressed to a Swedish correspondent his opinion that British party strife was merely a farce—not because the party policies were so similar, but because when the Opposition was defeated on any important issue 'it did not proceed to sabotage'.

The Communist Party of the Soviet Union is not, of course, a political party in the sense in which parties are understood by people who are not Communists. In 1917, though not yet counting on majority support, it suppressed all the other political parties in Russia, and the last thing likely in the most liberal possible future would be that other parties should be allowed to rise again. The Communist Party's task now is to govern the country and bring about Communism. It is meant to be an organizational and propaganda *élite*, spreading all over the country not only geographically but through branches or cells in every work unit and every other form of organization. Its work can appeal only to a minority, and most Soviet citizens are not members of the Communist Party. You cannot join simply by virtue of approving of Party aims and being willing to pay your subscription and attend a few meetings. The people wanted as members are Nature's organizing secretaries, trouble-shooters, club leaders, propagandists, and scoutmasters, and if you are not prepared to put your leisure and convenience entirely at the service of the Party, and to be sent away for months on special duties, you are unlikely to be accepted as a member. Once you have joined you cannot resign from the Party, though you may be expelled, and at intervals there have been mass expulsions of the careerists, the power-seekers, or 'those who joined because they couldn't do any other job', as I have heard Russians express it. Many people look down on Party members because of this element among them, or because they just do not like being chivvied, but some of the finest people in the country are also members and such people, especially if they are already popular among their fellows, are frequently pressed by the Party to join. Over the last twenty years or so the total Party membership has varied between about 3 per cent and about 5 per cent of the population, and this proportion is apparently thought satisfactory. The other 95-97 per cent describe themselves for political purposes by some such phrase as 'non-Party sympathizers'. Only Party members are normally referred to as 'Communists'.

However, this terminology should not be taken to imply that any large proportion of the Soviet people are privately out of sympathy with Communism. If a foreigner bluntly asks Soviet citizens what they think of Communism he will get one or two violently antipathetic replies (assuming the time and place of his question are discreetly chosen), but he would be unwise to attach much political significance to them. People who are opposed to Communism are in fact the very ones most likely to seek out a foreigner. But other persons, if approached, may point out that 'Communism' as Communists understand the term is a state of things to be reached in the future; it does not yet exist anywhere. 'Building Communism' is one of the most widely-used propaganda phrases, and it is a utopian slogan which seems to inspire a fair number of Soviet citizens.

To ask the ordinary person what he thinks of the present state of 'Communism' is too general a question altogether. He may approve of the new school his children attend, or the new goods in the shops; he may speak of sputniks or recall that Soviet power defeated the Germans (though he, like many Russians, privately feared that this could not happen); he may recall the seven price cuts since the war, or if he is old enough he may recall the village where peasants used to eat with their fingers from a common bowl and now, though living in the same huts, most of them have TV sets. On the other hand he may pass a sardonic comment, as an old peasant did to me in 1959, about his 'local Party secretary who misappropriated 30,000 roubles'; he may recall half a dozen friends who were hauled off to Siberia and died there, or the brutal questioning he had himself to endure from Soviet security police when his home town was recaptured by Soviet troops; or if he is an intellectual he may rail at the dogma he has to teach. He is surrounded by Communist features or features which have undergone Communist influence, but he has other things to think of than the quite theoretical possibility that an alternative 'system' might suit him better. He often has an idea that people in some Western countries are in many ways better off than Russians are, but 'one does not want to change one's mother for someone else's who happens to be more beautiful'.

It is most important for the foreigner to appreciate how universally the 'Communist' label is applied in the Soviet Union; it is used not only to describe the typically Communist features of the economic and political system, but also to describe attitudes—in the realm of morals, for instance—which may be almost identical with what is considered admirable by non-Communist peoples.

One may take an example from the world of education, where one of the dominant influences is that of the remarkable teacher Makarenko (1888-1939), a man who earned an international reputation for his success with colonies of delinquents, and a man whose humane educational methods could not but be approved by Westerners however anti-Communist. Makarenko says: 'I am deeply convinced that the quality of our Soviet personality is fundamentally different from that of personality in bourgeois society', but if one seeks in his writings for examples of 'Communist morals' to uphold this distinction one finds such illustrations as these:

The ideal example is the man who rescues someone from drowning and goes away without giving his name. What difference does it make if three or four people see you and applaud?

or

How often it happens that a man says of a woman who attracts him to a certain extent—'I am in love; I will give her everything.' But if he were accustomed to a proper exactness (*tochnost*) in his sensibility he would not have said 'I love you', but 'You attract me'. The absence of this subtlety is not far from the characteristic of a rogue or a swindler. *Tochnost* is our life—that is the moral norm.

Makarenko came from a working-class family, and when he says 'bourgeois' he is thinking of the class who kept him and his father down before 1917, and of the worst phenomena of later bourgeois society in other countries, which he learned about from his own press. His own standards came from the open good nature of the Russians among whom he grew up, and from his success in using empirical methods. He wrote two excellent books about his work with delinquents, and had little to say about formal educational doctrines until later in life, when he contrasted, as any Communist would, the moral attitudes which had become the official models during his own lifetime with the imperfect moral *practice* of Tsarist society as he knew it. Moral lapses in his own society he described in the Communist way as 'survivals' to be bred out by true, 'Communist', training, not as springing from perennially imperfect human nature. But in dealing with such lapses his own practice was the same as that of teachers of outstanding capacity in Western countries. One should surely feel it as encouraging for the future of Soviet society that Makarenko's lectures are recommended reading for Soviet parents as well as teachers, artificial though one may feel the distinction of 'Communist morals' to be.

It can be regarded ideally as 'Communist' to be sincere and discriminating when one is attracted by a woman, it is 'Communist' also to be loyal to wife or husband or respectful to parents—and it is 'Communist', too, to suppress all political opposition. Respect for the marriage tie or for parents, it would be said, is part of the basis of Soviet society, and to suppress political opposition must be necessary because, among other reasons, no other political system could secure the triumph of the moral values which, it is maintained, are so typically 'Communist'.

The Communist Party can thus attract the young by means of the moral image of a good Communist, as well as by the opportunities it can offer for social service, for vigilance against the capitalist foe, or for exercise of power. It attracts such people as the eager, smiling young peasant I met in a war-devastated town in the Moscow Region. He was delighted to be able to tell a foreigner how much he had read about the origins of the war, he was embarrassed at his dirt-ingrained hands, and he was torn between loyalty to the Party, which had given him confidential documents to carry, and an overflowing desire to prove, by showing these to me, that he was a trusted member of six months' standing. (His pride won the day and he shyly showed me the documents, though I was relieved to find that they only concerned matters which were already common gossip in Moscow.)

The Soviet Union owes much to the enthusiasm of such young men. But it is not surprising that more sophisticated citizens, without being at all anti-Soviet, may pay only lip-service to the Communist label and will turn away contemptuously from all the 'clenched-fist-in-air' type of propaganda. The nation in general has been outgrowing some of its naïveté, and one of the striking features of the recent political relaxation is that the whole business of banners and slogans is much less than it used to be, and the clumsiest kinds of propaganda are particularly reduced. Political formulations remain blunt, even savagely simple on the whole, but it is easier for people to ignore them than it used to be.

The relaxed conditions since 1956 or so are of the greatest interest for what they reveal or confirm about the Russian people, as well as for the possibilities which they have revealed in the Soviet system of government. It should be noted, however, that nothing fundamental has been changed in the Communist system of economic and political control; there is nothing in that system to guarantee that another Stalin might not arise, or that all the old machinery of police spying and labour camps might not be started up again. It seems rather unlikely that this would happen, because such good progress is being made without it, but the possibility is still there. People say nowadays that they believe the camps are almost empty, but they believe this only because they know so many people who have returned from them, or because they know former camp officials now doing other work. The Government did not make a public 'campaign' of emptying the camps; it did not report month by month how many people had been sent home, and it has never announced a total figure. Knowledge of Mr Khrushchev's crucial anti-Stalin speech has been allowed to filter widely among the population, and Mr Khrushchev has publicly said that there are 'almost no political offenders nowadays', i.e. that few people are now tried by the secret MVD methods. But the policy which sent millions of 'offenders' to camps as a result of such trials has not yet been openly repudiated or condemned. Meanwhile embassy telephones are still tapped, and students from America, Asia, and Africa in Moscow report that they are spied on and their contacts with Russians restricted.

However, there have been few if any executions for political offences since Beria was got rid of, and inefficient officials, or those who have pursued a mistaken version of the official line, seem nowadays to be punished only by fines, by transfer to another job of the same grade in less pleasant surroundings, or by demotion to a lower grade; legislation has in fact laid down a scale for these punishments.

The limits within which public criticism is permissible have also been much relaxed. Even Ministers are now criticized by individuals through the normal channels of the trade unions, the press, or Party branches. They may be criticized, that is, on the usual Soviet grounds of not having carried out policy adequately. But at lower levels popular opinion is being allowed to develop into what might be considered as a fragmentary criticism of policy itself, or even into suggestions for formulation of policy. This arises out of one of the Khrushchev reforms which promises to be most far-reaching in its effects—the regionalization of consumer goods production. 'The satisfaction of everyone's individual requirements' is one of the distant goals set by Khrushchev, and the regional organizations are responsible to the central government for providing the quantities and variety of most goods which may be locally needed. Previously people were much more at the mercy of centralized 'All-Union' Ministries, each responsible for the nationwide supply of a limited range of goods. The regional organizations are free to find out, and need to find out more precisely, what kinds and what qualities of goods local citizens need, and citizens have apparently not been backward in making known both their complaints and their wishes. So it seems probable that people's needs for, say, shoes in a particular region, and their rejection of certain kinds which are uncomfortable or wear out too quickly, may ultimately determine the quantity and quality of leather for which the regional authority makes itself responsible. This is a comparatively new approach for the Soviet economy, and it could mean, if the region were not one which itself produces leather, that the requirements of the local consumer could in the end affect the national plan.

Criticism might eventually reach a level at which it would have to be suppressed—if, for example, the leather supplied to the army were superior to that available to civilians, and people started to complain about this in public. But most Russians have too much political experience to be likely to make such an error. They will continue feeling their way, testing the limits of the new liberties sometimes to see if they are expanding, and happy to enjoy opportunities of discussion among themselves without need, probably, to fear the spy or the informer.

After the death of Stalin the brakes were taken off by degrees. It is significant that when Russians realized that the brakes were being released they did not react, so far as one can hear, by aggressive manifestations of individual behaviour, or demands for further political liberty, but rather by retreating thankfully into themselves or into family life. In 1959 and 1960 my own general impression was that people were simply happy at being able to relax. The only tendency which the Government might regard as dangerous has been the greatly increased curiosity about foreign countries, and the desire to travel abroad which one often hears passionately expressed, since the Government has now permitted this hitherto unthinkable indulgence to a few parties of selected citizens.

There is no longer the same pressing need to find ways of circumventing labour discipline; overtime is now discouraged, and one can change one's job easily if one wants. There is no longer any need to engage in *blat* to get any kind of food or drink, because supplies are at last plentiful and fairly well organized. People have so much more chance of acquiring the clothing or footwear they want, or a refrigerator or other consumer goods, that many of them, it is thought, measure their lives too much by material values. Dudintsev in his novel *Not By Bread Alone* defines a 'hero' by the characteristic, among others, that he does not 'acquire all the worldly possessions shown on the huge property-insurance poster pasted on the wall of his alley'. But Dudintsev himself is not free from the old Russian all-or-nothing attitude; he is probably somewhat too severe upon people's spendings. In 1959 a rather academic, not very self-indulgent friend put the new situation to me: 'For forty years,' he said, 'we have been asked to work for the future, for posterity, for our grandchildren, and now at last we are being asked to work for something which we can have in our hands *now*.'

Material prosperity will probably soften some of the old outlines of the Russian character. The contrast between feastdays and everyday, for example, is no longer so sharp, and Russian hospitality, though still lavish, is thus not quite so overwhelming as it has traditionally been; there is not the same need to overload the guest when his normal standard of living and your normal standard are higher. In general people seem to be a little more independent than they used, though personal relationships of all kinds are still developed and still verbalized much more than in countries such as Britain. It is a significant trait, I think, that so many Russians still seem incapable of doing two things at once. In 1960, as in 1934, it seemed to me that when the ordinary Russian is doing a job he has to give it the same wholehearted attention that he gives to a human being; the job seems so important to him personally that he grudges any division of attention. He can break off and talk to someone, but he finds it difficult to work and talk at the same time; he has to give his whole attention to the other person so that he can express himself at a proper Russian length and with a proper Russian intensity. 'They are still the same Russians,' said a Russian-born doctor, now a citizen of Israel, who was revisiting Leningrad for the first time in forty-seven years: 'The material progress is wonderful, the health service seems to me first-class, but my God how they can *talk*!'

So long as material prosperity continues to increase, and so long as control by the political police does not resume its old severity, the Soviet Government is obviously going to have much more popular support—more, probably, than it has ever had. People may demand still more liberty of criticism and still more voice in formulating the detail and sometimes perhaps the methods of policy, but one can scarcely hear of any evidence that they will demand a voice in determining basic policy, and there is no sign that the Government would yield to such a demand if it were made. People are so used to the machinery of the existing system that they will probably continue to accept it now that it is less unpleasant in its workings, as naturally as members of the Church of England accept their limited rights of lay discussion along with the authority of bishops whom they have no part in electing.

One may be sure that if the Soviet people demand more than this kind of share in government, or if the new regional liberties look like developing into too much autonomy, the Government will apply restrictions as severe as may be necessary. The great new feature of the Khrushchev régime—more significant even then the consumer goods—is that one drop of deviation is no longer held to corrupt the whole person of the deviator. This is a great relaxation compared with the attitude which has prevailed through most Russian history whether Tsarist or Communist, and the present Government must be watching eagle-eyed to see whether its trust is abused.

It will watch also—and the whole world will for different reasons watch—to see what kinds of individuals develop in the new atmosphere. The Government has always called for 'individuals'—people with special talents or skills, or special qualities of character or temperament, and educators such as Makarenko have always talked of developing such individuals in all their variety; but both Government and educators have meant individual members-of-the-community and not individuals-for-their-own-sake as they are understood in the West. There have always been measures intended to keep the more unusual personalities from straying too far from the communal fold, and to remind intellectuals that they too are servants of the nation. If increased prosperity brings out too many self-indulgent, lazy individuals or spoiled children the Government could resort to penal taxation or assign people to compulsory spare-time chores, it could shift some of them to unpleasant districts, or direct children into boarding schools. Such measures, however, are liable to generate their own growth of *blat*, and the Government will also expect results of a long-term nature from the increased permeation of society by the Communist Party. Partly as a reaction against the 'cult of personality' (i.e. Stalin), the role of the Party is being strengthened. One way in which this is done is by persuading more of the best men and women to become members, and by working through the traditional Russian methods of persuasion and social pressure whenever possible, in the hope of reducing self-seeking and of convincing people that, in the old Soviet phrase, 'the national interest and the interest of the individual are identical'. This is an approach which has always been used along with the more brutal methods, and in present circumstances more will be expected from it.

The solidity of the Russian community, and the old sense of Russia as a country with a special destiny, can provide a powerful cement between leadership and people. Mr Khrushchev is a Russian bred in Russian communal traditions, and it is noted with pleasure how he 'goes among the people', speaking impromptu and drawing on his store of peasant proverbs. Provided the Russian leadership remain sufficiently alert against the rise of another Stalin it is likely that the persons who reach the most powerful positions in the State will continue to be persons bred in old Russian traditions rather than the more analytic or independent types. In Russia as elsewhere the man who is going to the top in politics is usually a man who cares more for power than perfection, a man not of the most refined sensibility or perception, who is likely to take for granted as his conception of social relationships those of the mass among whom he was brought up.

The Russian community can arouse a good deal of fellow-feeling in Asians and Africans whose own tradition of social relationships is somewhat similar, and this is something not to be forgotten when the West is competing with Communism for the allegiance of 'uncommitted countries'. But visitors from countries such as Britain are usually more interested in the effects of Marxism on Russian society.

This book has been a social rather than a political study, and to discuss the Marxist outlook fairly would need much more space than I have. In concluding I should like to make some brief comments only.

The first is that if Marxism is to be judged by the success of the Soviet economy we are without the kind of evidence needed to arrive at a measured opinion. We may believe that a capitalist or social democratic government in the USSR would never have set aside such a painful proportion of the national product for capital investment as the Soviet Government has done. But this being done, we have inadequate evidence on which to judge whether or not progress might have been faster, more efficient, or more pleasant by capitalist or social democratic methods.

Quite apart from the desire to discover, for political reasons, which system might work better, it is something of a calamity for sociologists and economists everywhere that no one has yet been allowed to investigate in the Soviet Union, over several years and in proper detail, such matters as the following:

(a) A study of a single successful Soviet industry, to compare the efficiency of its use of manpower, materials, money, and research, and the satisfactions afforded to its personnel as well as to the consumer, with those of the same industry in say the U.S.A.

(b) The relative usefulness of targets and bonuses as incentives in Soviet industry.

(c) The problems and satisfactions arising from the employment of married women in a community where most married (as well as unmarried) women go out to work.

(d) Whether popular taste benefits permanently when people have no access to entertainment which exploits sensationalism, violence, and salacity, or whether if Soviet citizens were exposed to such entertainment they would fall victims to it.

If questions such as these could be properly studied the results even then could not be used as political evidence for or against Communism until a comparative study had been made of the questions in other Communist countries with different social and cultural traditions. The results nevertheless would be of world-wide interest quite apart from politics.

It is unfortunately most unlikely that the Soviet Government will grant facilities for foreigners to study such questions. They would refuse not only from a disinclination to have their weaknesses or secrets ferreted out. They would refuse also on ideological grounds; under their system human behaviour is not studied in this way. Their system has achieved great triumphs in man's mastery over nature, but to study the behaviour of men as a part of nature scarcely enters into their thinking. They have achieved a great deal for their people but seem comparatively uninterested in finding out what their people are like. There is no Soviet equivalent of David Riesman or William Whyte or

Abram Kardiner; no Soviet scientist would be likely to write on any such theme as 'the lonely crowd', or on the effect of industrial life in producing age-gangs, or in strengthening the role of the mother at the expense of the father. There is not, to the best of my belief, any Soviet work in the modern field of ethology—the study of the behaviour of both animals and men. It is not absolutely ruled out that such studies should be made, but the general effects of industrial society, in the main, are likely to be regarded as a matter of dogma.

The dogma says: 'Marx and Engels were naturally unable to detect the laws of development of Soviet society, since such a society did not exist at that time.' (*Bolshevik*, no. 15, 1946.) But unless there is to be a totally unexpected change in Communist practice it will continue to be the political leaders who will pronounce, *after the event*, on 'the laws of development of Soviet society'. It will be too dangerous politically for the sociologists to observe them first, and they are unlikely to receive any encouragement to do so. (If I am proved wrong in this forecast I shall be only too pleased.)

It may be maintained that the Soviet Government needed no help from sociology since its tasks were evident—to feed and clothe the people, to teach them to read and write, and to cure their diseases. But the upheavals produced in countries all over the world through coping with these simple needs have always brought about fresh social problems, and the Soviet Union has been no exception. Sociological observation and analysis, of the kind rejected by Communists, is in fact being carried out in countries such as India whose standard of living is below the Soviet standard, and as an adjunct to attempts to raise that standard.

The Soviet refusal comes from a fear of forsaking dogma but also, I think, from a natural fear of forsaking communal values which are taken for granted. To examine the nature of such values, as the educated public regularly do in Western countries, is dismissed by Marxists as 'metaphysics'. Their standpoint may be illustrated perfectly from their view of psychology, in which the unconscious is dismissed as 'mythical'. The psychologist Chernakov writes:

What self-respecting scientist can ignore qualitative differences between the psyche of normal people and that of the insane? Is it possible for a Soviet psychologist to follow in the footsteps of James and his followers in modern bourgeois psychology, who more and more take the position of ignoring the difference between normal and abnormal people and are ready to view the entire world as a lunatic asylum?

It would be anathema, apparently, to Soviet psychologists to suggest that the mentally abnormal may by their very aberrations throw light on the workings of the 'normal' mind—the mind of the person who is so formed by his community, perhaps, that he may be incapable of examining his own nature.

The enormous material progress in the USSR, and the proportion of the national effort devoted to technology, physics, mathematics, and chemistry sometimes lead Westerners to think of the Soviet Union as 'a scientific society'. But the Soviet attitude to the human and biological sciences indicates how far this is from being true. A truly scientific society would be one which tried to find out what kind of creatures human beings are in their infinite, and probably always infinitely possible, variety of individual and group—and which would put science, including social science, at the service of this variety. No such society exists as yet, but most of the thinking and research on lines necessary for such a society is being done in the United States, Britain, Holland, Sweden, and a few other countries; the Soviet Union is not among them.

In the West we believe on the whole (though some Westerners might be surprised to hear it) that people should so far as possible be allowed to learn by their own errors, that self-discovered truths, whether in politics, science, or the practice of everyday life tend to be the most valuable truths, and that it is worth while within very wide limits to let people question old truths for themselves; there may always be a new discovery as a result. We believe in a kind of inverted Gresham's law by which the logic of events must in the end cause people to hold on to sound ideas and drop unsound ones. The difficulties, wastage, and miseries which can arise from the liberal way of going about things naturally produce support for authoritarian movements from time to time, and Communism is not the first, though so far it is the most successful of these.

Communists believe in reference to authority as a short cut, and failure for them appears almost unmentionable. In Russia they have been able to develop these attitudes upon the old Russian bases of communal solidarity, restoration of the individual to the fold, and respect for arbitrary, unrepresentative government. They have been less able—though by no means totally unable—to provide outlets for the free and natural behaviour of individuals which was the other side of the old communal picture. Russians are going to take advantage of the individual opportunities offered under the new decentralization and the uneasy, limited relaxation of the intellectual climate, but by and large I think they will pursue their individual lines within a general and genuine loyalty to the community.

When it is proposed that international arms inspectors should operate in the Soviet Union without being responsible to the Soviet Government, Russians naturally react, as they did to the American spy plane, with an unsophisticated hostility which many nations would not show. They react in this manner because of the way in which their Government presents the issues to them, but also because of the degree to which they themselves identify their Government with their community. To diminish this kind of hostility or suspicion in either the Government or the people of Soviet Russia is going to be extremely difficult. On the other hand, one can safely prophesy that, when both sides are eventually prepared to make sacrifices for the sake of a better understanding between East and West, a fruitful and dependable element in that understanding will be constituted by the Russian capacity for human relationships and for life in the larger community.

Index